• Simon de Burton •

CLASSIC CARS

A Century of Masterpieces

ACC ART BOOKS

Contents

Alfa Romeo

This book is dedicated to my wife Helen and our children, Cosmo and Daisy, all of whom seem to share my enjoyment of travelling in and on old and defunct machinery.

Foreword
Robert Coucher

Founding Editor, *Octane* magazine

The term 'classic car' was arguably coined in 1973 with the launch of *Thoroughbred & Classic Cars* magazine. Prior to that, old cars were simply affordable bangers. The Vintage Sports-Car Club was founded in the Thirties by motorists who wanted to have fun in their old cars and this often meant taking a hacksaw to a boring saloon and converting it to a light, open 'special' to take on the aristos in their Bentleys and Bugattis.

Vintage cars (built before WW2) soon morphed into exciting sports cars in the Fifties and Sixties, when British cars were at their best. Simple rugged, good looking, often open and damn fun to drive, these classics were replaced by the drab, economical (oil crisis and all that), boring, rust-prone commuter cars of the Seventies – try thinking of a great sports car of that miserable decade – there's only really one – the Porsche 911. OK, the BMW CSi was good too, but that's about it.

Open sports car production reduced to a trickle as it was thought America was about to ban them entirely.

So, in the Seventies, car enthusiasts eschewed the lame eco-saloons and continued to enjoy sports cars of the Fifties and Sixties, so beginning the classic car movement where the classic car hobby became an industry. Cars were restored, parts were remanufactured, classic racing grew enormously, as did tours, shows and events around the world. In Britain today, it's estimated the classic car business is worth around £5 billion to the economy, as the appeal of old cars continues unabated.

Having grown up with old cars all my life – restoring, racing, crashing, driving and generally enjoying the challenge of running a daily classic, as well as being the editor of *Thoroughbred & Classic Cars* magazine before founding *Octane* magazine in 2003, I really get the classic car passion. But I'm still amazed that in our fast moving, hi-tech world individuals continue to love old-tech classic cars. Unlike forty-five years ago, modern cars are now rather good. Fast and economical, they have all the features needed to be on the pace – satnav, air-conditioning, automatic gearboxes, computer safety driving aids, even electric windows! Classics have none of that so they require proper *driving*, which, of course is the attraction. Modern cars are too easy and bland. You sit in the drivers' seat and do a bit of steering but that's about it.

Classic cars are involving specifically because they are *not* easy. They need care, understanding and patience – basically a close bond between driver and machine which is very rewarding when it gels.

In this book, Simon de Burton takes us for a journey through the evolution of interesting motor cars. He has astutely selected cars that we cannot fail to love, cars that we all want to drive and even possess. Simon's entries are full of fascinating nuggets, information and facts – many of which I didn't know – so I have been absorbed in the book. As someone who's been around the proverbial block quite a few times, I recommend this enticing and amusing read and it will certainly remain on my desk as an authoritative source of reference in the future.

Introduction

Karl Benz is widely credited with creating the world's first 'practical' automobile. It was on New Year's Eve, 1879 that he enjoyed his 'Eureka moment' thanks, in part, to his wife Bertha who had a nagging feeling that the engine, which had thus far eluded her husband's attempts to perfect it, might now be ready to co-operate.

"After supper my wife said 'Let's go over to the shop and try our luck once more. Something tells me it will go'," wrote Benz.

"So there we were, back again standing over the engine as if it were a great mystery that was impossible to solve. My heart was pounding. I turned the crank. The engine started to go put-put, and music of the future sounded with a regular rhythm. We both listened to it for a full hour, fascinated, never tiring of the single note of its song. The longer it played its note, the more sorrow and anxiety it conjured away from my heart.

"Suddenly the bells began to ring – New Year's Eve bells. We felt they were not only ringing-in a new year but a new era, which was to take on a new heartbeat..."

How right Benz was. Three years later, his new-fangled internal combustion engine, now further improved, was powering what the inventor advertised as an 'agreeable vehicle as well as a mountain-climbing apparatus.'

However, the general public was not the least bit interested. Until, that is, Benz's sons, Eugen and Richard performed an act that went on to become a rite of passage for youths around the world.

Together with Bertha, they crept out of the house and helped themselves to their father's contraption, not with the intention of climbing any mountains, but drawn by the realisation that here was a machine that offered something no one else seemed to have noticed – the potential for adventure. They instinctively realised that Benz's car could be used for far more than just pottering around the streets of Mannheim within a few hundred yards of where it was built, and boldly embarked on an expedition to the town of Pforzheim, more than 60 miles away.

Now this, surely, was what it was all about. Travelling at speeds that frequently approached a heady 10 miles per hour, pushing the car uphill and buying 'benzine' from apothecary shops along the way, the trio drove, cajoled, nursed and coaxed the Benz to their destination – it was the world's first motor tour and it caused the world to wake-up to the true potential of the automobile. Here was freedom.

By the close of the 19th century, development of the car had picked-up rapidly with marques such as Daimler, Benz, Peugeot, Panhard-Levassor, De Dion Bouton and Serpollet creating a variety of petrol, steam or electrically propelled vehicles.

The French, in particular, embraced the

automobile as a result of having inherited a ready-made structure of long, straight and well-surfaced roads that had been built for Napoleon's troops and, by 1903, the country was the world's largest producer of motor cars.

After that, automobile design progressed at a staggering pace to the point that, in 1907 no fewer than 40 entrants were able to put their vehicles forward to compete in the inaugural Peking to Paris race – although just five actually went through with shipping their cars to the start to take part in an event that had no rules and a prize that was decidedly modest in relation to the effort required: a magnum of champagne.

Typically, however, it was the necessity of war that proved to be the mother of automobile invention, with engineering lessons learned during the conflict of 1914–1918 resulting in the cars of the 1920s being vastly improved over their predecessors. The inception of the Le Mans 24 Hour race in 1923 and the decade's boom in properly organised and regulated Grand Prix racing in Europe that was led by Italy, Belgium and Spain also produced giant strides in performance and reliability.

And that is partly the reason why this book begins with cars that originated in the '20s and blossomed in the '30s – because, to many enthusiasts, these were the years when cars really changed from being relative rarities, owned by the fortunate few, to becoming, for better or for worse, an intrinsic part of society and key to the development of the 20th century.

I have been car (and motorcycle) mad for as long as I can remember, partly as a result of my mother's enthusiasm for both driving and automobile design that apparently filtered down to me and my two considerably older brothers. Even before I started school, they introduced me to the wonders of pre-war Rileys, post-war Bentleys and ex-war military vehicles that, at the time, were simply 'old cars' rather than 'classics'.

Indeed, it was not until well into the 1970s that the idea of 'classic cars' really took hold, and not until the 1990s when events such as the Goodwood Festival of Speed and the recreation of the Mille Miglia seemed to kickstart a new enthusiasm for old motors. Now that this has also been given a turbo boost by the intertnet, it has developed into a multi billion dollar global economy.

Now there are millions of classic car enthusiasts around the world and thousands of different models of classic about which they can 'enthuse'. What is interesting, however, is the fact that, wherever you go on the planet, there will be certain cars that every collector (or would-be collector) is especially keen to discuss, cars that, for one reason or another, have left a more indelible print in automobile history than others.

These are the ones that most car nuts would want to see if they opened up their garage doors to reveal an 'ultimate' collection – and many of them, I hope, form the basis of this book which comprises models that made their mark during the seven decades that span the 1930s to the 1990s.

Every one of these decades brought with it a significant advance in design and engineering, from the ground-breaking monocoque body of the Lancia Lambda and the supercharged engine of the Mercedes-Benz SSK first seen in the '20s, to the innovative front-wheel-drive of Citröen's Traction Avant launched in 1934 and the frugality and reliability of Volkswagen's democratic post-war 'Beetle'.

The 1950s, meanwhile, brought the brilliantly packaged Mini of the '50s and its Italian counterpart, the Fiat Nuova 500, with the '60s hailing the arrival of the Jaguar E-Type as the world's first, 150 mph production car.

Even the oft-maligned 1970s produced its gems in the form of the now legendary Range Rover and the giant-killing Lancia Stratos rally car, while the subsequent decades saw the arrival of Audi's four-wheel-drive Quattro, the futuristic BMW M1 and, of course, Gordon Murray's simply staggering McLaren F1 which heralded the arrival of the modern-day supercar.

But, while eye-wateringly valuable cars such as the F1, the Ferrari GTO and the Jaguar C Type are all coveted by the majority of classic fans, most also have a soft spot for more affordable, less performance-orientated models that are widely regarded as offering just as much driving fun and aesthetic appeal as their far faster, rarer and more expensive counterparts. This is why this book also features the Land Rover, the military Jeep, the Mini Moke and the MGB, as well as the Datsun 240Z, the Citröen DS and the Morgan 4/4.

All are cars with that certain *je ne sais quoi* that makes them appealing to enthusiasts simply for what they are, rather than for what they are worth or for the speed that they can achieve.

There is no doubt, of course, that many readers will quickly notice marques and models that are missing from this book that they might regard as glaring omissions. If that is the case, I apologise – and hope that such critics will acknowledge that most of us only have a finite amount of space in our garages. Even our fantasy ones.

In any event, changing times suggest that we may not be able to enjoy any of these old-fashioned, fossil-fuelled cars made from nuts, bolts, steel and ingenuity for very much longer, as touch screens and invisible electronic wizadry make ever greater inroads into our lives (even to the point that we might not even be required to drive anymore).

Hopefully, however, books such as this will remain in existence long enough to enable future generations to marvel at the strange contraptions in which we used to travel during the 20th century – even if they can never quite convey the full spectrum of fun and frustration they caused us in equal measure.

5·50-18
RACING

1930s

Alfa Romeo 6C 1750 Gran Sport

Production dates: 1929 - 1933
Number built: 257
Designer: Vittorio Jano
Engine: 1750cc, straight six, supercharged. 85 - 102 horsepower
Fuel consumption: 20 mpg
Top speed: 84 - 110 mph

Alfa Romeo's glorious '6C' is a fitting car with which to start our trip through the automotive decades, not simply because it begins with 'A', but because it epitomises the 1930s sporting automobile. The 6C was actually introduced in 1927, but it was at the dawn of the 1930s that the car became really interesting because, by then, its original 1500cc engine had been replaced by the far more powerful 1750cc unit. In 'top of the range' Super Sport and Gran Sport guises, it was available with twin camshafts and a supercharger.

Typically of the era, 6Cs were usually sold as a rolling chassis for which buyers would commission coachbuilders such as Zagato and Touring to create bodywork, which was often of the open-topped, two-seater variety.

The 6C's brilliance can be attributed to a young engineer called Vittorio Jano who had been recruited to Alfa Romeo by the then-manager of its racing team – none other than Enzo Ferrari. Jano's work on Alfa's P2 grand prix car filtered through to the road-going models, most notably the 6C 1750 – the most exciting of which was the Gran Sport variant introduced in 1930.

Featuring a distinctive, raked-back radiator for better water cooling and an American-made Roots supercharger, the car produced 85 horsepower and a level of performance that made it unbeatable as a road-going racer in major sporting events such as the RAC Tourist Trophy and Italy's gruelling Mille Miglia.

Although capable of nudging 100 mph (this was in 1930, remember), the 6C 1750's greatest asset was not (and is not) its top speed but the way it feels. Although its four-speed gearbox can be challenging to those lacking a suitably deft touch, it is otherwise a car that seems remarkably ahead of its time, with light steering and crisp, predictable handling that encourages spirited driving.

When fitted with classic sports bodywork – the aforementioned open, two-seater effort by Zagato is quintessential – a 6C 1750 is, quite simply, the epitomy of the 1930s Italian sports car. Add to that the thrilling sound of its howling supercharger at peak revs and the throaty rumble of its exhaust (best in side-mounted form) and a better expression of 'la dolce vita' on four wheels is difficult to imagine.

In total, 257 Gran Sport cars were completed, just 12 of which were so-called 'Testa Fissa' ultra high-performance models with fixed cylinder heads. Among Alfa Romeo enthusiasts and lovers of pre-war sports cars in general, however, there are few people who would not wish to open the doors of their motorhouse to find any 6C sitting inside with its top down and its windscreen folded flat, quietly waiting to take its owner back to the golden years of drivers such as Tazio Nuvolari, Giuseppe Campari and Achille Varzi.

Belissima!

Alfa Romeo

Jaguar SS100

Production dates: 1936 - 1940
Number built: 214
Designer: Sir William Lyons
Engine: 2.6 or 3.5 litre
Fuel consumption: 20 mpg
Top speed: 100 mph

The Swallow Sidecar and Coachbuilding company was founded in 1922, but the 'SS' abbreviation by which it was known came to have unfortunate connotations due to the initials being shared with the Nazi's notorious Schutzstaffel – by then, however, Swallow co-founder William Lyons had been inspired to introduce a new name. "I immediately pounced on Jaguar," he said, "as it had an exciting sound to me."

The marque didn't become known simply as 'Jaguar' until 1945, but it had already been adopted to describe SS's high-performance offerings with the introduction of the SS100 in 1936 – which was also the first car to wear the now famous 'leaping cat' mascot.

Elegant and beautifully proportioned, the £395 SS100 was the company's first true sports car and formed the basis of Jaguar's on-going reputation as a maker of surprisingly affordable cars that – as the slogan went – offered 'grace, pace and space'.

The latter was not in abundance, however, in the two-seater SS. Aimed at the sportsman, it featured a 102-inch wheelbase combined with a 2.6-litre, straight six engine that had been breathed upon by tuning expert Harry Weslake who developed a twin-carburettor, overhead-valve cylinder head that endowed the SS100's Standard-based powerplant with 104 horsepower (rising to 125 horsepower for the enlarged, 3.5-litre version introduced in 1938).

In either capacity, it was sufficient to give the car a genuine ability to broach 100 mph (hence the 'SS100' name) and helped to make it a favourite among competition drivers. One of the first people to realise its potential was motoring journalist Tommy Wisdom who, with his wife Elsie navigating, unexpectedly trounced the previously all-dominant Bugattis to win the Alpine Trial within months of the car's launch.

As a result, SS100s were fielded in some of the most prestigious and demanding races of the day, including the Mille Miglia, the Targa Florio and the RAC Rally, acquitting themselves admirably on a regular basis.

One SS100 that became notable for its remarkable originality was, however, used for a decidedly non-sporting purpose. It was bought new by an owner who chose it because he wanted a car that was sufficiently narrow to fit between the rows of hops on his Kentish farm. He used the car for 'hop checking' for several years before it was parked in a barn and forgotten about, only being exhumed after his death in the early 1990s.

Other than having one crushed headlamp as a result of a roof beam brought down during the 'great storm' of 1987, it was found to be entirely original and was sold at auction for £100,000 to the late Glen Kalil, an oriental carpet dealer – who, much to the admiration of the classic car community, chose to simply dust-off and polish the SS100, replace its bent headlamp and drive it as found.

Perhaps the most celebrated of all SS100 owners, however, was the late Tory MP Alan Clark. He bought his first while still at Eton and went on to 'have one in the garage for nearly my entire motoring life.'

Among many epic drives in his SS100s, Clark recalled a one-hit run from London to Skye 'helped by the midnight sun,' sliding into a Portuguese ditch while 'duelling' with a 1948 Ford and racing the eccentric Ottoman millionaire Nubar Gulbenkian's chauffeur-driven Buick from Estoril to Sintra.

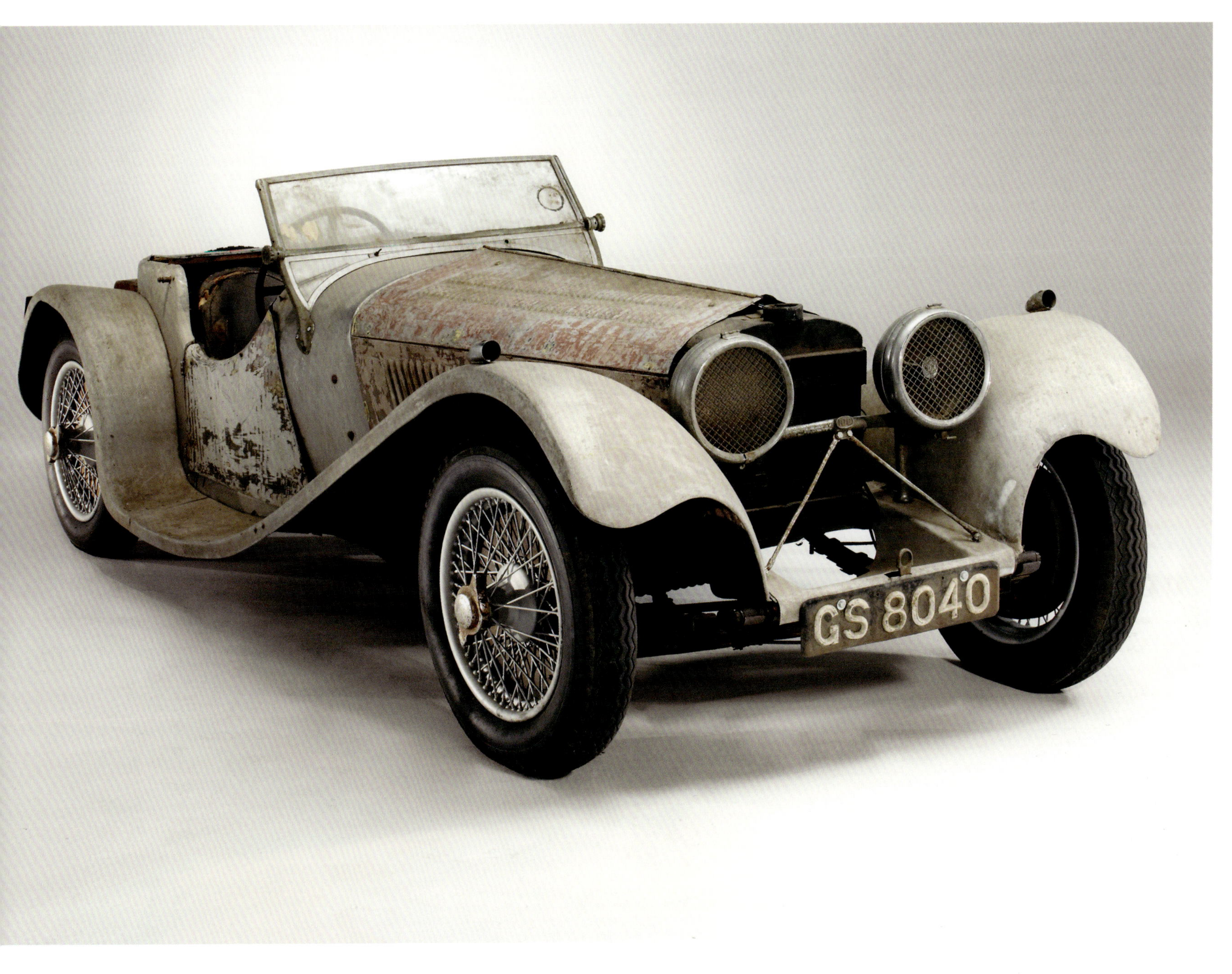

“The chauffeur wasn’t really up to it and I expect the wind, in every sense, affected the passengers”.

Alan Clark MP

SS 100

DUNLOP RACING
SS
100

Rolls-Royce 20/25

Production dates: 1929 - 1936
Number built: 3,827
Designer: Unknown
Engine: 3,669cc, six cylinder
Fuel consumption: 15 mpg
Top speed: 75 mph

Introduced in 1922, the Rolls-Royce '20' was the first of the celebrated marque's designs to be aimed at the owner-driver rather than the traditional plutocrat whose natural position was on the back seat rather than behind the wheel.

The car proved popular, offering Rolls-Royce kudos at a slightly lower price than previous models – but many buyers missed the point and burdened the rolling chassis they were supplied with by commissioning coachbuilders to create overly weighty bodywork that blunted the relatively modest performance of the car's 20 RAC-rated horsepower.

Rolls-Royce addressed the situation in 1929 with the introduction of the upgraded 20/25 model (i.e. a car based on the '20' but with a 25 horsepower engine). It was a smart move, the 20/25 becoming the marque's best seller during the important inter-war years. Due to events such as the Great Depression, this era saw many other luxury automobile firms fall by the wayside.

More than 3,500 20/25s were built and, thanks to that legendary Rolls-Royce engineering, more than 2,500 of those survive today in various forms – and the variety of those forms is extensive.

The extra power met with some buyers' desire to have a 'fully loaded' Royce with elaborate limousine bodywork and a sumptuous interior built by firms such as Hooper, Barker, Freestone and Webb or Gurney Nutting (to name but a few). But the 20/25 was at its best when fitted with a small sedan, coupé or two-seater set-up that kept it light and fleet of foot, although it could never be described as a 'sports' car.

Indeed, one of the attractions of the 20/25 today is that it can be found in so many different guises, each of which imbues the car with a different character. Many survivors are, to be frank, decidedly bland, box-shaped saloons which, but for having the famous Rolls-Royce radiator at the front, could have been made by any one of dozens of manufacturers.

Those fitted with more exotic two-seater and drophead coupé creations – often by overseas coachbuilders such as Million Guiet or Gangloff of France, Brewster of America and Carrosserie Worblaufen of Switzerland – can be of a fabulous appearance that belies the steady-going, dependable engineering underneath.

It is this steadiness and dependability that makes the 20/25 an essential component of any serious classic collection, not least because these cars are easy and enjoyable to drive with their high-geared steering and tough, quiet engines. Yet the ubiquity of the 20/25 also makes it the most affordable of all pre-war Rolls-Royces and one which is easy and inexpensive to maintain. In other words, it's the perfect combination of prestige and simplicity.

JJ 6339

Lancia Lambda

Production dates: 1922 - 1931
Number built: 13,000 across nine series.
Designer: Vincenzo Lancia
Engine: 2,121 - 2,569cc, V4, overhead camshaft.
Fuel consumption: 20 mpg
Top speed: 75 mph

Although it was introduced at the London and Paris motor shows as far back as 1922, Lancia's brilliant Lambda was way ahead of its time, reaching its zenith with the eighth and ninth series models (introduced in 1929 and 1930 respectively) which represented the ultimate expression of what was already a remarkably advanced design.

Undoubtedly one of the greatest cars ever produced, it was built from the ground up, rather than being simply an improvement on what had gone before.

To that end, the Lambda featured an avant-garde, monocoque construction which did away with the traditional chassis/ bolt-on body arrangement, making the car stronger, more rigid, quieter and smoother; it introduced 'sliding pillar' front suspension in place of archaic leaf springs; the propellor shaft was housed in a tunnel running the length of the car's centre, meaning it could be lower and more aerodynamic; the front and rear bench seats served as stressed members to help rigidity; and the engine's 'V4' arrangement was so compact that the gearbox could be mounted beneath the bonnet.

Unlike most cars of the era, the Lambda's monocoque design meant the standard, open-top 'torpedo' bodywork could not be changed on early models – instead, Lancia offered bolt-on tops which enabled owners to convert their cars to saloons or the more extravagant 'sedanca de ville' style, while independent coachbuilders created further elegant designs for the upper body.

By the time the seventh series cars appeared in 1927, however, a new, separate chassis had been engineered with a stiffness equal to that of the monocoque, making for a greater choice of coachwork. It was also the inaugural year of the Mille Miglia - and privateers drove Lambdas to fourth and fifth places, encouraging Vincenzo Lancia to develop a competition car by shortening and lightening an early Lambda to create a 'Sport Spyder' model.

The apotheosis of the Lambda, however, was the ninth series model of 1930 – considerably longer than its forebears (especially on the optional 'long chassis') it was a large and imposing car which offered the potential for effortless long distance touring thanks to its comfort and powerful 'Tipo 79' engine of 2.6 litres, which was tuned for low-down pulling power.

But the ninth series proved to be short lived, as Lambda production ceased in 1931 with the car being replaced by not one, but three different models, each designed for more specific types of driving. All were excellent in their own way – but their existence served to demonstrate just what a consummate all-rounder the pioneering Lambda had really been.

And that shape. Once seen, never forgotten...

Citroën 'Traction Avant'

Production dates: 1934 - 1957
Number built: 760,000 across three main models
Designers: Andre Lefebvre and Flaminio Bertoni
Engine: 1,303cc - 1,911cc, four cylinder and 2,867cc six cylinder
7 - 15 horsepower (French fiscal rating)
Fuel consumption: Up to 30 mpg
Top speed: 70 - 85 mph

The French Citroën company has always been renowned for its ability to innovate – and had been running for a mere fifteen years when it produced one of the most progressive motor cars of the twentieth century in the form of the Type 7A or '7CV'. Not everyone recognises that designation, but even those with little more than a passing interest in automobiles might be familiar with the words 'traction avant' by which the 7A and the models that succeeded it (the 11 and 15CV) are better known.

The car's 'traction avant', or 'front wheel drive' was, perhaps, its stand-out feature at a time when convention dictated that cars should be pushed from behind rather than pulled from ahead, and it was highly significant. The arrangement not only gave the car a lower centre of gravity and outstanding road-holding, it allowed for a flat floorpan that was integral to the monocoque design. As on the Lancia Lambda that had gone before, it dispensed with a conventional chassis in favour of a fully stressed body.

The 7CV and its variants also offered all-round independent suspension (a vast improvement on conventional leaf springs) and, another 'first', hydraulic brakes. To ease maintenance and repairs, the engine and transmission could be quickly removed from the front of the car as a single unit. Yet earlier models were not without their inconveniences – such as a boot that could only be accessed from inside.

What was most remarkable about the Traction Avant, however, was that André Citroën set out to mass produce such a high specification vehicle – and that is exactly what he achieved, churning out more than three quarters of a million during the 23-year production run of the three different models, with large numbers being built at a factory in Slough, England (where they were known as the 'Light 15', 'Big 15' and 'Big Six', the latter denoting the six-cylinder engine of the 15CV).

Regardless of where a Traction Avant was built, however, the car still called 'the Queen of the Road' in France remains as much a symbol of the country as garlic and the striped Breton jersey – not least, perhaps, because it was famously driven by the pipe-puffing fictional detective Jules Maigret and always seems to feature in any portrayal of the French Resistance.

The good news for retro-lovers, however, is that the large number of survivors means Traction Avant ownership is still relatively affordable, save for rare versions such as the two-door sedan and cabriolet, nine-seat 'Familiale' and 'hatchback' Commerciale which are additionally sought after and command high prices.

Duesenberg Model J

Production dates: 1928 - 1937
Number built: Around 200 (including supercharged 'SJ' and short wheelbase, supercharged 'SSJ').
Designer: Fred Duesenberg
Engine: 420 cu in/6.8 litre straight eight, 265 horsepower (more if supercharged)
Fuel consumption: 10 mpg
Top speed: 119 mph

It's the dawn of the 1930s, you're a super-rich American playboy with money to burn and a reputation to build. What do you drive? No contest – a Duesenberg, of course. Because Duesenberg was America's outspoken answer to Rolls-Royce, founded by German émigré brothers August ('Augie') and Frederick Duesenberg and, eventually, financially backed by millionaire entrepreneur Errett Lobban Cord.

Cord already owned Auburn and the eponymous car maker of his own founding, but he saw in Duesenberg the opportunity to build the ultimate in automobiles. Duesenburgs already had a 'name, the brothers having launched their first passenger car in 1919 and achieved outstanding success on the racetracks – but the firm was in dire financial straits, making Cord's offer to buy it outright in 1926 decidedly welcome.

Fred Duesenburg's first job was to design a car that could out-do the most extravagant creations of exotic high-end marques such as Hispano-Suiza, Isotta-Fraschini and Mercedes-Benz and, after a couple of false starts, the Model J was conceived in 1928.

A huge, 420 cubic inch/6.8 litre engine with twin camshafts and 32 valves produced 265 horsepower and sat in a chassis that, alone, was priced at $8,500 – the equivalent of almost $120,000 today.

At first Cord couldn't sell them quickly enough to tycoons such as Howard Hughes, William Randolph Hearst and the Whitneys. But then the 1929 Wall Street Crash stopped the party and just 200 Duesenbergs were ultimately built before the great man's automobile empire fell apart in 1937.

Among those 200 cars, however, were some truly spectacular creations – not least the Whittell Coupe supplied to the eccentric and wildly wealthy Captain George Whittell in 1931 as a rolling chassis costing $17,000 (at a time when a Ford Model A could be had for just $400).

Bodied by coachbuilder Murphy, it featured a brushed aluminium roof detailed to mimic the closed fabric top of a convertible (complete with faux mechanism); upholstery trimmed in gleaming black patent leather; a thickly-chromed fuel tank; port and starboard running lights; an underside painted crimson; and secret compartments to stash illegal alcohol.

Whittell drove it just ten thousand miles in eighteen years before giving it away – but the car returned to the spotlight in 2011 when it fetched $10 million at auction.

More recently (and more representative of true Duesenburg values), a Model J 'disappearing top' Torpedo Convertible bodied by Murphy realised $3 million, while in 2013, another made $4.5 million.

But examples of this truly extraordinary marque rarely appear for sale – so be sure to snap up the next one you see...

GX - 9527

Bentley 'Blower'

Production dates: 1927 - 1931
Number built: 55 (5 race cars, 50 road cars)
Designers: W.O. Bentley/Tim Birking/Amherst Villiers
Engine: 4,398 cc, four-cylinder supercharged producing 175 horsepower in road trim, 240 for racing
Fuel consumption: 12 mpg on the road, as little as 4 mpg in race conditions
Top speed: 120 mph

Bentley established itself as the default choice of motor car for the wealthy sportsman during the 1920s but, as the first half of the decade passed, the power of the old, three-litre engine simply didn't cut the mustard on the race tracks against the emerging breed of high-performance machinery being produced by rivals such as Mercedes-Benz, Bugatti and Alfa Romeo.

By then, ailing fortunes had forced marque founder Walter Owen Bentley (W.O.) to hand-over control of the company to wealthy customer Woolf Barnato, who was inspired to invest in the business by the 1924 Le Mans win achieved by fellow 'Bentley Boys' John Duff and Frank Clement. By 1927, some of Barnato's cash had enabled W.O. to develop a new, four-and-a-half litre engine using a four-cylinder version of the existing six-litre 'six' which was already proving successful in competition.

Barnato won Le Mans in 1928 in a four-and-a-half litre car and again in both 1929 and 1930 in six-cylinder Speed Six models – but another Bentley Boy, Sir Henry 'Tim' Birkin, believed supercharging the four-and-a-half-litre would result in the ultimate racing Bentley.

The often dogmatic W.O. spluttered at the prospect but, lacking financial clout, was powerless to stop the project once it was approved by Barnato – although, as creator of the four-and-a-half litre engine, he was able to veto any intrinsic alterations to its design.

As a result, Birkin went ahead (with the financial help of eccentric benefactor Dorothy Paget) and commissioned engineer Amherst Villiers to produce an initial batch of five racing Bentleys with Roots-type superchargers – the first example being based on a three-litre engine – which ran off the front end of the crankshaft and were attached to the car in a frame mounted ahead of the radiator grille.

In total, 55 such 'Blowers' were produced in order to comply with the requirements of entry to Le Mans. However, despite their engines' power being boosted from a normally aspirated 110 horsepower to as much as 240 horsepower in competition trim, the supercharged cars never won a single race (which no doubt gave W.O. a certain degree of pleasure).

Blowers did, however, achieve success in speed trials but were never as reliable as the 'standard' four-and-a-half which had a well-deserved reputation for being robust and over-engineered.

Their rarity and reputation as the supreme British sports car of the pre-war era means, however, that values have soared to as much as $4 million – although perhaps the greatest endorsement of their status as the ultimate gentleman's possession came when author Ian Fleming made a custom-built Bentley Blower the transport of choice for James Bond in the novels *Casino Royale*, *Live and Let Die* and *Moonraker*...

VN 4270

VN 4270
GB

Austin Seven

Production dates: 1922 - 1939
Number built: 290,000 (home market)
Designer: Herbert Austin
Engine: 747cc, four-cylinder, 10 - 33 horsepower
Fuel consumption: Up to 50 mpg
Top speed: 50 - 100mph for competition versions

After America had its Ford Model T and before Germany had its Volkswagen, Britain had its own 'people's car' in the diminutive form of the Austin Seven.

Company founder Herbert Austin recognised a potential market for a small vehicle that would compete with both the growing number of motorcycle and sidecar combinations and the generally crude 'cyclecars' that had become the main types of motorised transport accessible to the less well-off family, envisioning what he described as 'a real car in miniature'.

Back at the 'works' his concept fell on stony ground. Undetterred, he converted his home billiard room into a drawing office and, with the assistance of a young draughtsman, designed the Austin Seven.

The car first hit the streets in the summer of 1922 and was unashamedly basic, with a simple A-frame chassis, a 747cc engine and a braking system in which a foot pedal operated the rears and a hand lever operated the fronts.

Even after it had entered production, the Seven was still considered something of a joke at the Austin factory. The breakthrough came when aviation pioneer Gordon England and Austin's son-in-law gathered together a band of drivers who wanted to compete in speed events in Sevens, bringing the car into the public eye and demonstrating its undeniable all-round competence.

The initial price of £225 announced in July 1922 was reduced to just £165 by the end of the year. With winter underway, the orders came flooding in and the cyclecar market virtually evaporated overnight.

Soon, the Seven became available in various guises, such as the Brooklands Super Sports – a replica of the record-breaking, lightweight two-seater built by England; the equally sporty Ulster; the open-topped Chummy (the original); the box saloon; the van; and a special version re-bodied by the Swallow coachbuilding company. Additionally, the Seven design was licensed to car manufacturers around the world and, by the end of production in 1939, 290,000 had been built and sold in the home market alone.

'This little car, which can be run for about a penny a mile, is an ideal car for a woman to use herself, enabling her to do more shopping without fatigue, to visit her friends more frequently, and to attend social and recreational functions', ran the spiel in language characteristic of the era.

'Another appeal is to the businessman, as it enables the executive to make the utmost use of his time, whilst his expenditure is no more than it would be on tram or bus fares, and there is no need to point out the value of such a car for the commercial traveller, who can penetrate into districts that poor train services would make it hardly worth his while to cover otherwise.'

It sounds just like the sort of car we could do with today...

U 2667

Austin
Seven

Citroën 2CV

Production dates: 1948 - 1990
Number built: 3.8 million
Designer: Jean-Pierre Boulanger
Engine: 375cc, 425cc or 602cc, air-cooled, flat twin
Fuel consumption: 50 - 90 mpg
Top speed: 40 - 71 mph

For a long time the butt of jokes among those of more extravagant automotive tastes, Citroën's 2CV (or 'deux chevaux' for 'two horsepower') is now widely recognised as one of the greatest creations in the entire history of car design.

Its roots can be traced back to the 1930s when Citroën vice president Pierre-Jules Boulanger set about developing a car that would revolutionise the lives of French farmers by providing them with a vehicle that was economical to buy and run, had light off-road capability, was simple to fix and could carry four people and a decent load.

By 1939, a batch of 250 pre-production cars had been built featuring twin-cylinder, 375cc water-cooled engines, aluminium bodywork, an ingenious linked suspension system and a fabric roof that folded down to the rear bumper to enable the transport of unfeasibly large objects.

But all plans to produce the 2CV commercially were shelved following the outbreak of WWII, at which point the completed vehicles were either destroyed, disguised or hidden to prevent them falling into Nazi hands, lest the design was adopted as the basis for a versatile military vehicle.

The 2CV project was, however, resurrected in 1948, having lain dormant for almost a decade. By then, the need for an inexpensive small car which would mobilise the rural folk of France was even more necessary – but a shortage of materials post-war meant the already austere, original design had to be pared down even further.

Engines became air-cooled, bodywork was made not from aluminium but from thin steel (with bonnet panels being corrugated for strength) and the spartan specification offered but a single tail light, one windscreen wiper, a dipstick to check the fuel level – and any paint colour, so long as it was grey.

To the average farmer, however, the 'umbrella on wheels' offered a giant leap forward when compared to a horse and cart. Despite having a top speed of just 40mph, the 2CV proved an instant commercial hit with 1949's modest production run of fewer than 900 cars rocketing to more than 6,000 within a year.

By 1952, output had exceeded 20,000 per annum before peaking at 168,000 in 1966. But while the 2CV gradually gained practical additions such as a twin rear lights and windscreen wipers, an illuminated speedometer, an exterior driver's door lock, a glass rear window and a larger 425cc (and then 602cc) engine, its *raison d'être* (as the French like to say) remained resolute: it was, and always would be, a small, light, practical car designed for the masses.

What few could have expected, however, was that the bargain basement 2CV would come to be regarded as being synonymous with a carefree, happy way of life – not least during the 1970s and '80s when they were made available in a range of bright colours and special editions, such as the orange and white 'Spot', the red and white 'Dolly', the blue and white and the maroon and black 'Charleston'.

However, as safety standards became more stringent and drivers' expectations grew, the 2CV's flimsy bodywork, 'deckchair' seating and outdated performance resulted in the last Portuguese-built examples rolling off the line in 1990.

For years afterwards, second-hand 2CVs could be picked up for a song. But now, with all things retro being entirely on-trend and many people calling for a return to a simpler way of life, they have become collectors' cars that, ironically, only the relatively wealthy can afford...

Bouncing along, Tigger-like, on their pliant suspension, the cars became the very symbol of French 'joie de vivre'.

CITROËN

Volkswagen Beetle

Production dates: 1945 - 2003
Number built: 21.5 million
Designer: Ferdinand Porsche
Engine: 1100cc/1200cc/1300cc/1500cc/1600cc air-cooled, flat four
Fuel consumption: 25 - 40 mpg
Top speed: 60 - 80 mph

Some might say that the only good thing Adolf Hitler ever did was to instigate the creation of the now-legendary Volkswagen Beetle. He kicked the project off in January 1933 after being made Germany's chancellor, part of his master plan being to develop a comprehensive road network that would be constructed by the mass unemployed.

With the 'autobahnen' programme underway, Hitler turned to the country's leading automotive designer, Ferdinand Porsche, to create a 'car for the people' – a 'Volkswagen' – that would cost less than 1,000 Reichsmarks (RM), could reach 60mph and cover more than 40miles on a gallon of petrol.

Hitler also stipulated that the car should have an air-cooled engine, which was conceived not by Porsche but by an Austrian engineer called Franz Xavier Reimspiess whose designs were nothing if not sustainable. He also penned the form of the Volkswagen badge which prevails to this day.

After five Zundapp-based prototype cars had been rigorously tested (two of which were built in Porsche's home garage), the Volkswagen became a state-funded project backed by RM 50,000 of government money. This saw a series of 30 more experimental vehicles being produced – called VW30 and with the now-familiar 'beetle' bodywork – that were put through their paces by a team of drivers hand-picked from the SS.

The final design was signed-off in 1938 and featured the addition of the rear window that the VW30 lacked, running boards and a one-piece bonnet in place of the original split design.

Soon afterwards, work began on building a factory to produce the cars 50 miles east of Hanover beside the Mittelland Canal, and Hitler announced that the VW would be officially named the Kdf-Wagen, or the 'Strength Through Joy Car'. Not so joyous, however, was the subsequent decision to make it available only by signing-up to a hire purchase agreement requiring a minimum weekly payment of RM5, with delivery being made only *after* the full RM990 price had been paid off.

As with the Citroën 2CV, however, KdF-Wagen production was thwarted by the outbreak of war. Instead, the underpinnings and powertrain of the car were used as the basis for a military vehicle called the Kubelwagen, more than 50,000 of which were built between 1940 and 1945.

At the end of the conflict, the KdF-Wagen factory came within the British military zone and received a visit from representatives of the UK's Society of Motor Manufacturers and Traders who, despite being impressed by the rather bomb-damaged facility and this odd-shaped 'people's car', concluded that it 'is not to be regarded as an example of first-class modern design to be copied by the British industry'.

What probably saved the Beetle, however, was the fact that there was a serious shortage of transport in post-war Germany leading (ironically) to a request from the British Army for 10,000 cars. The German Post Office also placed a large order and, under the management of Major Ivan Hirst of the Royal Electrical and Mechanical Engineers, more than 7,500 Beetles were built in 1946 alone.

The running of the plant was subsequently taken over in 1948 by former Opel executive Heinz Nordhoff who introduced improvements to the Beetle that increased its export potential. Following initial sales in Holland, it began to be sold in America and then around the world with manufacturing plants being set-up in South Africa and Brazil during the 1950s and Mexico in 1964.

The rest, as they say, is history: save for alterations in engine capacity, the introduction of various trim levels and thousands of small improvements, the Beetle remained more or less the same throughout a 58-year production run that ended in 2003 after a staggering 21.5 MILLION examples had been built.

So, it really was a ‘people’s car’ after all.

FLORIDA
01-16
BV6 716
ANTIQUE

Alle 10000 km auswaschen

Land Rover

Production dates: 1948 - January 2016
Number built: 2,016,933
Designers: Maurice and Spencer Wilkes
Engine: A variety of petrol and diesel engines, including 1600cc, four cylinder petrol; 2.25 litre, four cylinder petrol; 2.6 litre, six cylinder petrol; 3.5 litre, V8 petrol; 2.5 litre, five cylinder diesel and 2.4 litre, four cylinder diesel
Fuel consumption: 15 - 35 mpg
Top speed: 50 - 90 mph

As Maurice Wilks and his brother Spencer were strolling along Anglesey's Red Wharf Bay in the summer of 1947, one of them picked up a stick and sketched in the sand their vision for an agricultural vehicle that might take the Rover car company in a new direction after the war.

Maurice was Rover's technical chief and Spencer its MD. They owned a farm on Anglesey, around which they used to drive an ex-Army Jeep. Competent though this was, it inspired them to try to make something better that would be both worthy of the Rover name and capable of traversing all types of terrain – and the idea for the Land Rover was born.

After tinkering about with a Rover-powered Jeep and experimenting with the short-lived idea of a centrally positioned steering wheel, the brothers eventually settled on a vehicle with an 80 inch wheelbase, a 1600cc petrol engine producing 55 horsepower, a four-speed gearbox and permanent four-wheel-drive. A shortage of steel led to a decision to use plentiful aluminium for most of the body panels and, in June 1948, the first production Land Rovers began to roll off the line at Rover's Solihull plant.

Priced at £450, the car was intended as a stop-gap vehicle to bring the company some much-needed cash from overseas, but it proved unexpectedly popular and the initial production run of 100 per week was quickly ramped up to 500.

The design evolved gradually, with the original, 80 inch wheelbase growing to 86 inches and then 88 inches; longer (107 inch and 109 inch) versions were introduced; the 'Series 1' became the 'Series II' in 1958 and prevailed in modified 'IIA' and 'III' form for thirty years, before the cart spring suspension was replaced with coil springs on the '90' and '110' models of the early 1980s that were the basis for the ultimate 'Defender'.

The model was finally phased-out at the end of 2015 after more than two million had been produced, during which time Land Rovers in their various forms had been used as everything from military vehicles to camping cars, had carried explorers to some of the most remote places on earth, had helped to save lives as ambulances and put out blazes as fire trucks. Land Rovers have even been converted into mobile coffee shops and ice cream vans.

In short, the Land Rover had proved itself to be one of the toughest, most versatile, most long-running designs in automotive history – and certainly one of the most loved.

But none of that could alter the fact that the ultimate 'Defender' variant was little changed from the Land Rovers that had gone before, meaning it simply didn't cut the 21st century mustard in terms of safety, performance and driver comfort.

No sooner had news emerged of its imminent demise, however, than values of Land Rovers old and new began to rocket, with the two millionth Land Rover off the production line being auctioned by Bonhams in London for a remarkable £400,000. Special edition 'Autobiography', 'Heritage' and 'Adventure' models were even bought and mothballed as investments.

Most true Land Rover lovers, however, would balk at the idea of owning a 'Landy' that doesn't wear a generous coating of mud with pride and carry a healthy assortment of battle scars, each with a story to tell.

LAND ROVER
HUE
166

HUE
166

HUE
166
LAND ROVER

Willys Jeep

Production dates: 1941 - 1945 (original models)
Number built: 637,385 (original models)
Designer: Karl Probst
Engine: Four-cylinder, 2.2 litre 'Go Devil'
Fuel consumption: 10 - 20 mpg
Top speed: 65 mph

In early 1940, in anticipation of its inevitable entry into WWII, the U.S. Department of War invited 135 motor manufacturers to tender their designs for a light, all-terrain, four-wheel-drive reconnaissance vehicle that was sufficiently versatile to be adaptable for a range of uses.

However, so tight was the brief and so short the time frame that a mere two firms submitted viable pitches: Willys-Overland and American Bantam, with Ford being kept in the wings in case its vast production capacity was needed.

Initially, American Bantam landed the job and commissioned designer Karl Probst to conceive and present a suitable prototype, which he did within the Department's prescribed deadline of 49 days – the result being the Bantam Reconnaissance Car that went on to become known simply as the 'Jeep'.

More than 2,700 BRCs were made, with most being dispatched to the British Army – but American Bantam's inability to build the large numbers required resulted in the blueprints for the design being handed to Willys-Overland and Ford in order that full-scale production could get underway.

Measuring 132 inches long and 62 inches wide, the Willys MB (for 'Military B', the Bantam product being 'Military A') was powered by a punchy, 2.2-litre, four-cylinder 'Go Devil' engine that was famously reliable and produced almost 60 horsepower, giving it a top speed of around 65mph.

Weighing a mere 896 kilos (Willys lightened the original AB design by more than 100 kilos), the Jeep – as it was unofficially named – had impressive acceleration and, when the going got a bit too rough, was light enough to be manhandled out of tricky situations.

By late 1941, the Jeep had made itself invaluable and the need for large numbers lead to both Willys and Ford being contracted to produce them, with the two firms both having input into the final design and building more than 637,000 between them before the end of the war in 1945. (Ford also built 13,000 amphibious versions that were – inevitably – dubbed 'Seeps').

Despite the widespread recognition of the Jeep name, its origins are something of a mystery. Some say it was derived from the letters 'GP' used for Ford versions, and others that it was a term favoured by U.S. Army mechanics to describe new types of vehicle. It may even have been inspired by Eugene the Jeep, a jungle pet owned by cartoon character Popeye.

In any event, it proved to be a name that would never go away. Immediately post-war, Willys created a civilian version called the 'CJ' (Civilian Jeep) – although military models were pressed back into service within a few years, this time to serve in the conflict zones of Korea and Vietnam, where they proved as effective as ever.

For years afterwards, military Jeeps continued to be built under licence in countries around the world, notably in France as the Hotchkiss M201 which remained in production until 1960 and was used by the French Army until the 1980s.

USA
194076
1△-82R-A-3

FIRST

Morgan 4/4

Production dates: 1937 - present
Number built: 7,000 (approx.)
Designer: H.F.S. Morgan
Engine: Original car - 1,122cc Coventry Climax four cylinder; Latest model - 1,595cc Ford Sigma. 5 litre, five cylinder diesel and 2.4 litre, four cylinder diesel
Fuel consumption: 25 - 50 mpg
Top speed: 80 - 110 mph

The present-day Morgan 4/4 is instantly recognisable as having evolved from the original 4/4 created by H.F.S. Morgan in 1936 – making it the longest-running car design in history.

The '4/4' of the title refers to the fact that this particular Morgan has both a four-cylinder engine and four wheels. Back in 1936, this represented something of a giant evolutionary step for the tiny, Malvern-based manufacturer which, until then, had focused on producing three-wheel 'cyclecars' powered by exposed, v-twin engines.

The prototype 4/4 was first seen on Boxing Day 1935 when 'HFS' – an engineer who established his eponymous car marque in 1909 at the age of 28 – competed in the London to Exeter trial and gained a premier award in the class for experienced or 'veteran' competitors.

It was to be the first of many competition successes for the new four-wheeler, production versions of which featured an ash framework and an 1122cc Coventry Climax engine driving through a four-speed gearbox, initially supplied by Meadows and later by Moss.

Wins in events such as Ireland's Ulster Grand Prix and Leinster Trophy demonstrated the car's sporting potential and prompted an advertisement that read: 'Morgan made their name in the three-wheeler world and captured every prize worth having – and here is a four-wheeler, four-cylinder car that bids fair to capture the plums in the sporting circles of the motor car world. An 80mph sports – and its price is only £210.'

That competition success combined with the affordable price made the car popular with dashing young men of the day and the 4/4 – along with MG's TC – quickly came to be associated with army officers and RAF pilots who, being quintessential English gentlemen, would drive them hard but could always be depended upon to slow down in the presence of horses, vicars and ladies on bicycles.

Between 1936 and the outbreak of war three years later, 663 two-seater 4/4s were built and sold, together with 99 of the less sporty – but more practical – four-seat versions along with 58 drophead coupés. Unlike the original, fully open, two-seater, the coupé offered the luxuries of fixed side windows and a more nifty folding roof mechanism.

But it was when post-war production re-commenced in 1946 that the car demonstrated that there could be a future for a design that was, essentially, already out of date. The 4/4 has since evolved into today's version which, despite being the entry-level model in the Morgan line-up, is regarded by many as the purest expression of the original, pre-war car made suitable for 21st-century life. Powered by a 1595cc Ford Sigma engine, it will easily top 100mph yet is capable of returning a frugal 50mpg.

Virtually devoid of electronic devices and with a framework that's still made from sustainable ash wood, the 4/4 still offers a true, seat-of-the-pants driving experience that is becoming increasingly difficult to find among today's resolutely high-tech automobiles.

Classic? The word could almost have been invented for it.

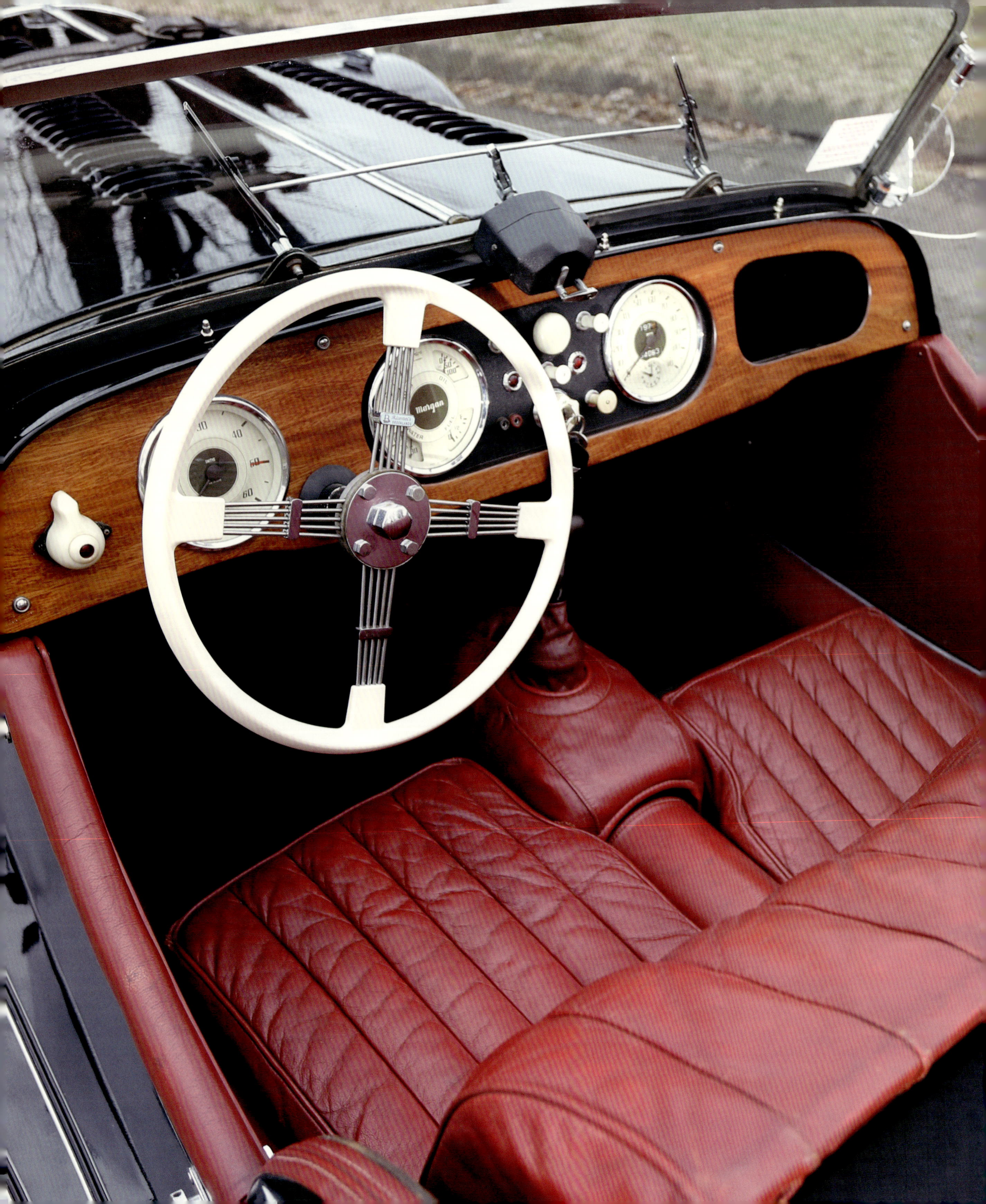
Morgan

Chrysler Town and Country

Production dates: 1946 - 1949
Number built: 8,373
Designer: Paul Hafer ('woody' bodywork)
Engine: Eight cylinder, 5.3 litre
Fuel consumption: 10 - 15 mpg
Top speed: 95 mph

When Chrysler launched its Town and Country model in 1940, it was in the form of an imposing, wood-clad station wagon capable of carrying eight passengers and all the luggage they could muster – as the name suggested, it was a car for those who were sufficiently wealthy to have a weekday life in town and a weekend one in the country.

By 1942, the requirements of war meant an end to 'T and C' production and the name lay dormant until 1946, when it was reinstated, not on another large station wagon but this time as a luxury sedan or convertible, each based on Chrysler's New Yorker chassis.

The wood, however, remained to form a striking feature of this decidedly decadent car that represented an unashamed celebration of a return to normal life post-war.

Pekin Wood Products of Helena, Arkansas, supplied the timber which was shipped to Chrysler's plant in Jefferson Avenue, Detroit, in order to be meticulously hand-formed to the curves of the steel bodywork – a painstaking and time-consuming process that accounted for a significant portion of the Town and Country convertible's steep, $3,220 price tag. In all likelihood, this helped the car attract the patronage of stars such as Clark Gable and Bob Hope.

The mahogany panels with white ash frames (which would later be substituted for more cost-effective Di-Noc decal imitations) clad the car's doors and trunk, which was set-off by a pair of specially designed, art deco-style tail lights that were unique to the model.

When it came to the car's interior, however, it was a case of 'no veneer in here'. The dashboard was a symphony of dazzling chrome and Bakelite, with chunky, push-button radio controls, celluloid door winders and rectangular instruments that further invoked an art deco vibe, while plush seats promised a magic carpet ride for driver and passengers alike.

With the increasing number of women drivers in mind, Chrysler created an upholstery options list as long as the car itself, offering a variety of materials ranging from soft leathers to corduroys, tweeds, plaids and tartans that made it possible to create a virtually bespoke interior precisely to madame's requirements.

That important notion of smooth progress was enhanced by a steering wheel boss decorated with the Chrysler wings and stamped with the words 'Fluid Drive' – the name given to the liquid coupling fitted between the engine and transmission that made it possible to glide to a halt in any gear without dipping the clutch, and also made the car virtually impossible to stall.

On the open road, meanwhile, the 5.3-litre, straight-eight motor that produced 135 horse-power at a lowly 3,400 revs-per-minute made for the sort of effortless progress that could take one from 'town to country' without breaking sweat in the slightest. Although, with a dry weight of almost two tons, this was neither the most nimble of cars nor the most frugal.

When it came to making a statement the Town and Country was up there with the best of them. And boy, could it keep up with the Joneses...

212
35

Chrysler
Town & Country
PANEL LIGHTS
READ LIGHTS
TEMP CONTROL
DEFROST
HEATER FAN

Allard K1

Production dates: 1946 - 1948
Number built: 151
Designer: Sydney Allard
Engine: Eight cylinder, 3.6 or 3.9 litre
Fuel consumption: 15 - 20 mpg
Top speed: 90 mph

London-born Sydney Allard was a natural engineer whose love of motor cars lead him to start racing a Morgan three-wheeler in 1929 at the age of 19, later progressing to a series of Ford-based specials of his own design with which he achieved competition success in everything from sand racing to trials, sprints and rallies.

During the war, Allard ran a repair shop that specialised in renovating Ford Army vehicles – a business that thrived and resulted in him employing more than 200 people. However, his passion always lay with building high-performance cars, usually by combining powerful, large-capacity engines with lightweight chassis in a formula that would later be adopted by Carroll Shelby, a one-time Allard racer who went on to create the celebrated Shelby Cobra.

With time on his hands post-war, Allard set about using his large supply of left-over Ford parts to develop a two-seater sports car with a box-section chassis, transverse leaf springs, distinctive open bodywork – and, of course, a punchy, American V8 engine. His first effort, the J1, was made available as a pure competition car or as a two- or four-seat tourer, with the former variant being offered only to people who would campaign it and, therefore, demonstrate the performance that put Allards among the fastest-accelerating cars of their day.

Allard's next effort, the K1, was intended purely for the home market and, as such, was available only in right-hand-drive form. It cost £850 and combined a 106-inch wheelbase (six inches longer than that of the J1) with the option of a 3.6-litre or 3.9-litre Ford V8 giving speeds of up to 90mph and, like the J1, blistering acceleration.

Although bordering on the ugly from the front, the K1's silhouette was undeniably attractive, while its rear-end was more hot rod than tourer. All the same, its well-appointed interior and high-torque engine made it a serious mile-eater and 151 were built. Today, there are only an estimated 21 surviving, of which 11 are in the US, where Allards became popular after the 1950 launch there of the competition-orientated J2.

For many, however, the K1 remains the quintessential, road-going Allard two-seater that combines quirkiness with rarity, performance and a degree of versatility that makes it capable of tackling the muddy hills of a trials course, the smooth Tarmac of a race circuit or the circuitous roads of an alpine rally.

Although the Allard motor company went bust in 1958, Sydney Allard's automotive genius is remembered to this day – as are his remarkable motoring exploits, which include winning the Monte Carlo Rally at his first attempt, taking third in the 24 Hours of Le Mans and in 1962, at the wheel of his self-built dragster, recording the then-fastest quarter mile time ever posted in the UK.

He died in April 1966 at his home in Sussex, eight years after his eponymous firm went bankrupt – and, eerily, on the very night that arsonists set fire to the dormant Allard factory in London's Clapham.

SMT 26

MG TC

Production dates: 1945 - 1950
Number built: 10,001
Designer: Cecil Kimber
Engine: Four-cylinder, 1250cc
Fuel consumption: 28 mpg
Top speed: 70 mph

Founded in 1924, MG (Morris Garages) established a reputation for making nimble, two-seater sports cars that found favour with the more dashing young men of the era and, during WWII, became more or less the default choice of ground transport for every style-conscious pilot in the Royal Air Force.

William Morris was in the bicycle business before he branched-out into the automotive world with the famous 'Bullnose' of 1913 which was sold from a converted stable block in Longwall Street, Oxford – the original Morris Garage, which became the Morris Garages after being extended in 1913.

But it was sales manager Cecil Kimber who really developed the competition character of the MG marque, starting with the £175 MG Midget M-Type of 1928 that introduced a line of sports cars that continued until 1955.

The first Midgets to offer really good performance 'out of the box', however, were the T Types which went into production in 1936 in the form of the 1292cc-engined TA, a tiny machine with a distinctive, rear-mounted fuel tank and doors with scalloped tops intended to provide a comfortable resting place for elbows when they demanded relief from being squashed into the cramped interior.

The TB of 1939 offered a tougher, 1250cc engine – but the outbreak of war meant that only 379 examples were produced before the Abingdon factory was turned over to war work, meaning it wasn't until 1945 that arguably the most important T Type model of all was launched, the £527 TC.

Although available only as an open, two-seater of very similar appearance to the TB (it was, essentially, a stop-gap model), the new car arrived at exactly the right time, in as much as it faced little competition and had the potential to satisfy a ready appetite in America for just such a small, affordable, fun-to-drive sports car.

Of the 10,000 produced, many went to the US where they are often credited with having helped to kick-start the country's craze for motorsport, not least because the TC's standard, 54 horsepower engine was highly tunable and relatively tough.

One of many examples of the Midget's giant-killing potential relates to a car owned by long-time *Autosport* photographer George Phillips who bought his TC new in 1947, mildly tuned the engine and then finished second in class at the Brighton Speed Trials.

Spurred on by his success, he then fitted a lightweight body and achieved fourth places in the Manx Cup, Ulster Trophy and 12 Hours of Montlhéry of 1948 – after which he entered the tiny car for the Le Mans 24 Hours.

Despite being disqualified on his first attempt in 1949, Phillips took the car back the following year and completed 1,760 miles at an average speed of 73mph to finish second in class behind a far more powerful, works-entered Jowett Jupiter.

Although admittedly highly modified with an aluminium body (according to Le Mans regulations) attached to a lightweight framework, the car was still a TC at heart – and, as Phillips proudly explained afterwards, the car used "no water, 1 pint of oil, got around 24 miles to the gallon, and [was] still on the original tyres".

What more could anyone ask for?

EAM645

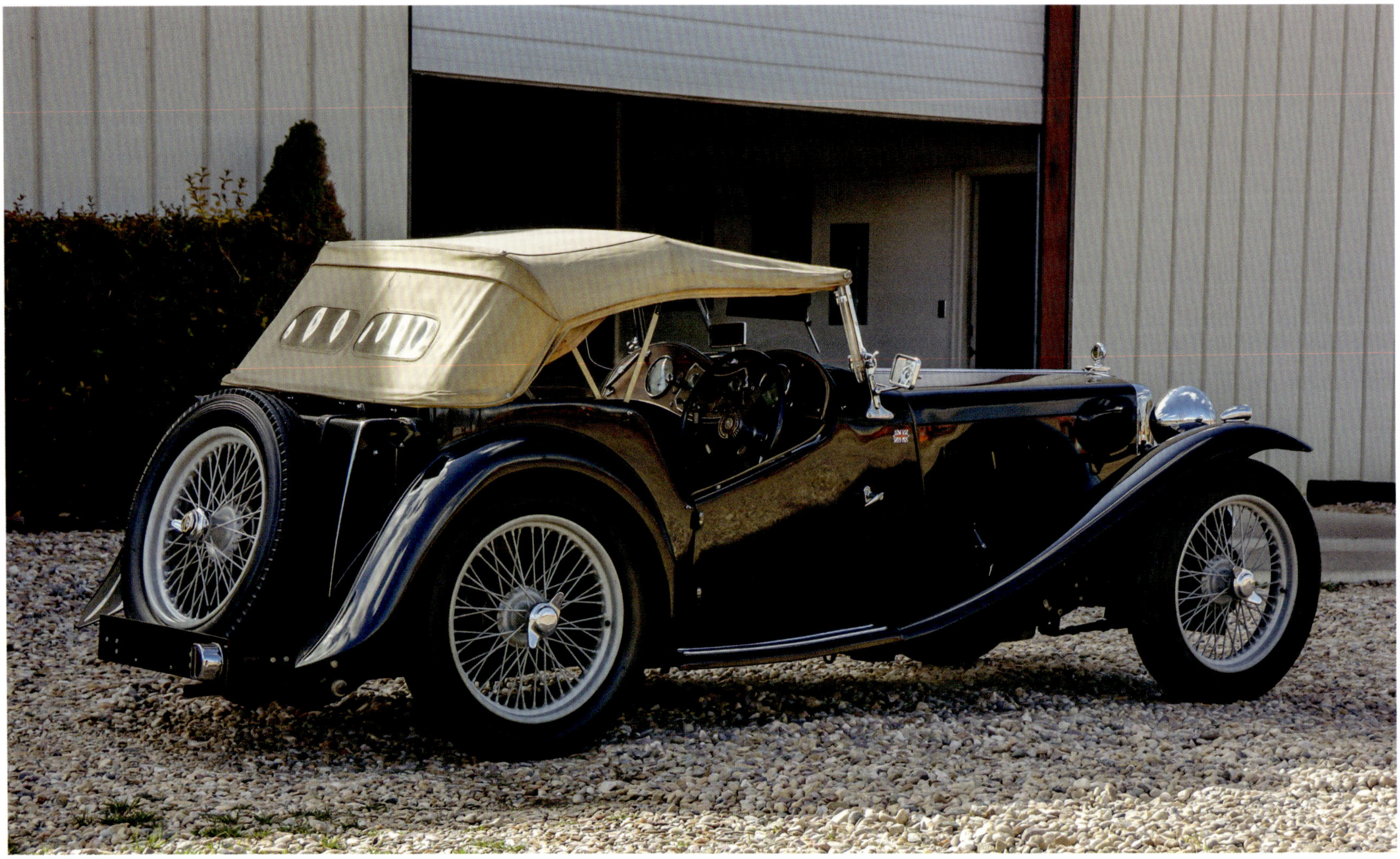

MG

1950s

Jaguar C-Type

Production dates: 1951 - 1953
Number built: 53
Designer: Malcolm Sayer
Engine: 3.4 litre, twin camshaft, six cylinder.
Fuel consumption: 10 - 15 mpg
Top speed: 140 mph

Jaguar's history might date back to 1922 when the firm was founded as the Swallow Sidecar Company, but it was not until 1950 that the marque first showed promise in competition. Leslie Johnson – a furniture maker, prodigiously talented driver and close friend of Jaguar founder William Lyons – drove an XK120S to third place at the Le Mans 24 Hours before clutch failure forced the car's retirement with just three hours of the race to go.

Despite failing to finish, Johnson's demonstration of the XK's potential was sufficient to encourage Lyons to instigate the creation of a car that was built for racing from the ground up. The result was the decidedly beautiful XK 120 C, which came to be known simply as the 'C-Type'.

The new car featured a lightweight, tubular steel space frame draped in aerodynamic, lightweight aluminium bodywork penned by former aircraft designer Malcolm Sayer. The long, swooping bonnet concealed a version of the 120's engine with a new cylinder head, high-lift camshafts, racing pistons and an 'open' twin-pipe exhaust system that increased the output to around 200 horsepower.

The C-Type's competition focus negated the need for road car conveniences, so there was but a single door and no boot lid, the curvaceous rear deck sitting atop a vast, 39-gallon fuel tank which, even at racing speeds, enabled the car to run for almost 400 miles without re-fuelling.

The racing obsession with saving weight meant the interior was spartan – although the car's twin bucket seats were carefully designed to provide long-distance comfort during the type of endurance events for which it was intended.

An initial three C-Types were built for use by the Jaguar factory team and made their debut at Le Mans in 1951. One of them, the car driven by Peter Walker and Peter Whitehead, achieved victory becoming the first British car to win the gruelling event in close to 20 years.

Despite failing to repeat the performance the following year, 1953 saw the factory enter another team of three C-Types which were the first Le Mans competitors to feature new-fangled disc brakes. The car driven by Tony Rolt and Duncan Hamilton duly snatched a second, sensational victory for the marque.

In total 53 C-Types were built, 43 of which are believed to have been sold to Jaguar customers. Most were used for competition, regularly being driven to circuits, raced and then driven home again (often bearing the scars of battle).

Production ceased in 1953 with the D-Type successor arriving the following year – but C-Types continued to prove effective in competition for some time afterwards, both in short circuit races and long distance road events.

Their tractability, power and reliability made them popular with drivers who simply wanted a fast and exhilarating road car. Those same traits, combined with a glorious racing pedigree, eligibility for the world's most prestigious historic race events and, of course, that beautiful shape, have made the C-Type one of the most coveted of all classic sports cars. As a result, on the rare occasions when examples appear for sale, they fetch big money.

One that raced at Le Mans in 1953, for example, was sold for £8.4 million when it crossed the auction block in 2015, while 2017 saw the sale of the first example to be imported into the US (and the first to win a race there) for more than £3.7 million.

Not bad for a car that originally cost little more than £2,000...

19
19
LFS 672

41

19

LFS 672

Austin-Healey 100/100-6/3000

Production dates: 1952 - 1968
Number built: 80,000
Designer: Donald Healey
Engine: 2.6 litre, four-cylinder/2.6 litre, six cylinder/3.0 litre, six cylinder
Fuel consumption: 20 mpg
Top speed: 110 - 120 mph

It's not known who first used the term 'hairy chested' to describe certain British roadsters from the 1950s and '60s which offered seating for two, large-ish engines and plenty of 'grunt'. But ask any gathering of classic car enthusiasts to name the model with the hairiest chest of all and they'll likely say 'Austin-Healey'.

The brainchild of Cornish polymath Donald Healey, the original 'Healey 100' was unveiled at the Earls Court Motor Show in 1952 as an affordable, mass-market offering intended to bring the financially ailing Donald Healey Motor Company into the black after a series of more expensive, low volume sports cars had failed to make money.

Healey hit on the idea of using the engine and some of the running gear from the existing Austin A90 Atlantic, a car which Austin chairman Leonard Lord believed would boost the marque's sales in America but ultimately proved unappealing due to its odd looks and general mediocrity.

But once installed in a gorgeous, low-slung, two-seater body penned by Healey's brilliant designer Gerry Coker, the Atlantic's 2.6 litre, four-cylinder engine provided sufficiently sparkling performance to justify the 'Healey 100' designation – in recognition of its top speed of over 100mph.

No sooner had the wraps been pulled off the exciting new car at Earls Court, than Lord set about negotiating with Healey to produce it at Austin's Longbridge factory, giving rise to the celebrated 'Austin-Healey' marque – and resulting in no fewer than 14,634 '100s' being built between 1953 and 1956, together with 55 higher-performance 'S' versions.

There followed the '100-Six' with a 2.6 litre, six-cylinder engine, which grew to become the '3000 MKI' and 'MKII' and, ultimately, the '3000 MKIII', all of which were available both as two-seaters and in less popular 'two-plus-two' guise.

The more luxurious later cars benefited from wind-up windows, fold-down hoods and full-sized windscreens. By the time production of such so-called 'Big Healeys' came to an end in 1968, around 80,000 had been sold across the five main variants, with 75 per cent being exported to America.

In the hands of celebrated 'works' drivers such as Pat Moss, Paddy Hopkirk and Jack Sears, Austin-Healeys achieved a string of podium finishes in competitions including the Monte Carlo, Liege-Rome-Liege and Mille Miglia rallies. Factory-backed cars also took part in the Le Mans 24 hours and major US events such as the Sebring 12-hours and the Carrera Panamericana.

These days, a good survival rate, those superb looks and that impressive competition history have resulted in the Austin-Healey becoming one of the best-loved of all classic British sports – a fact that has sent values for top-tier 'standard' models soaring from around £30,000 a few years ago to as much as £80,000 today. In 2011, however, an ex-works 'special test' car that competed at Le Mans in 1953 realised a record £843,000.

802 UYN

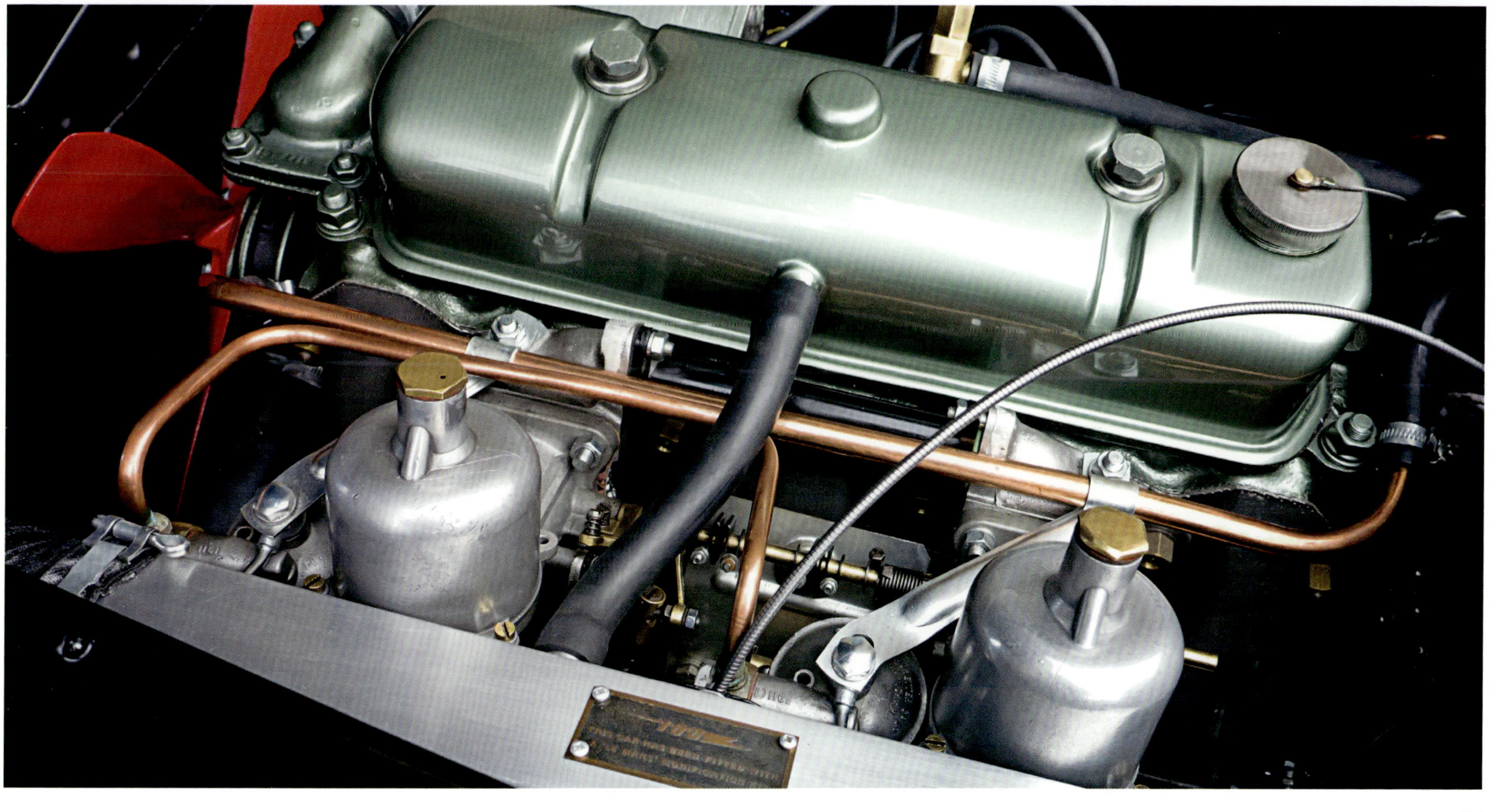

Porsche 550 Spyder

Production dates: 1952 - 1968
Number built: 92 (not including RS60 and RS61)
Designer: Ferdinand Porsche
Engine: 1,498cc, twin overhead camshaft, four cylinder
Fuel consumption: 20 mpg
Top speed: 136 mph

If you subscribe to the belief that small is beautiful, there's a good chance you'll appreciate the Porsche 550 Spyder. Completed in 1953, it was the first purpose-built racing car to be designed by the German firm and, when compared with its contemporaries manufactured by the likes of Ferrari, Maserati and Jaguar, it seemed far too diminutive to possibly pose a threat in competition.

But within months of its unveiling, the 550 had already earned an unofficial moniker: 'the giant killer'. The first victory came at the car's inaugural outing, the Eifel Races held at the Nurburgring in May 1953; then followed first and second in class at Le Mans a few weeks later; a first in the 1954 Carrera Panamericana; a first in class at that year's Mille Miglia (after Hans Herrmann drove beneath a railway-crossing barrier to make up time); and a decisive win in the 1956 Targa Florio when Umberto Maglioli came in ahead of the second-placed Maserati by a remarkable 15 minutes.

The 550 (Porsche's 550th design project, between 549, a truck transmission, and 551, a three-speed gearbox) was designed by Ferdinand Porsche using the same mid-engined configuration he had created for the mighty Auto Union prewar grand-prix racers. Available first in 550 guise with a flat, welded, tubular chassis, it was upgraded to a spaceframe as the 550A; the majority of cars used a 1,500cc, four-cylinder, four-camshaft engine which produced 110 horsepower.

The fact that the aluminium-bodied 550 weighed a gossamer-like 590kg meant that it boasted a top speed of 136mph and the type of delightful handling that enabled it to leave larger, far more powerful cars in its wake on the narrow, twisty roads of events such as the Targa Florio. However, the production span of the 550 proved to be a relatively short four years, with the final 550A models being completed in 1957 before giving way to a more sophisticated successor, the 718 RSK (although variations on the Spyder called the RS60 and RS61 remained available, in tiny numbers, until the early 1960s).

The ninety-two original 550s built were largely dispersed throughout Europe and America, with the most famous US-export model being number 55 – aka 'the Little Bastard' – the car in which Holloywood idol James Dean died while driving to the Salinas road races in 1955.

In recent years, however, even 550s without such Hollywood provenance have soared in price. An example in excellent, original condition that might have cost around £250,000 a decade ago would easily command 10-15 times that figure today. Although it is worth mentioning that another screen star, the comedian Jerry Seinfeld, sold his 550 in 2016 for $5.35 million...

Despite the high value of the cars, many owners compete in them on a regular basis. Most do so simply because a well-sorted 550 is as much a pleasure to drive today as it was when new in the middle of the last century.

Spyder

PORSCHE

Austin/Morris Mini

Production dates: 1959 - 2000
Number built: 5,387,862
Designer: Sir Alec Issigonis
Engine: 848cc, 970cc, 997cc, 998cc, 1,071cc, 1,098cc, 1,275cc. All four-cylinder
Fuel consumption: 30 - 45 mpg
Top speed: 75 - 110mph

Although the celebrated Mini is perhaps best known as an icon of the 1960s, it first burst onto the motoring scene in 1959 having been created by the late, great Sir Alec Issigonis, a Turkish-born, British national who had already made his mark on automotive history through his creation of the Morris Minor more than a decade before.

After designing the Minor, Issigonis worked for Alvis before being taken on by the newly formed BMC (British Motor Corporation) shortly before the Suez crisis of 1956 that caused a sudden, and decidedly serious, international petrol shortage.

The situation led BMC chairman Sir Leonard Lord to postpone the firm's existing projects in order to focus on designing an all-new economy car that would be frugal but also practical, comfortable and nippy.

Assigned with the task, Issigonis calculated that a 'package' measuring 8ft 9in in length, 4ft 2in in width and 4ft 4in in height would result in about the smallest possible interior that could carry four people and luggage, with the true stroke of genius being to mount the mechanicals transversely at the front and have them drive the front wheels. Alex Moulton, meanwhile, invented the brilliant and compact 'rubber cone' suspension system that enabled a tiny, 10-inch wheel to be placed literally 'at each corner'.

The little car was unveiled to the press in April 1959, with 2,000 being built in advance of it becoming officially available to buy four months later in nearly 100 countries around the world. Initially under the Austin or Morris marques, there were various model designations before the 'Mini' name became official a couple of years later.

In the same year, a souped-up version of the car tweaked by racing car designer John Cooper was launched, featuring an engine enlarged from 848cc to 997cc, twin carburettors, a close-ratio gearbox and front disc brakes. It quickly proved itself to be highly competitive in rallies and saloon car races.

Even more powerful and capable 'S' versions were subsequently introduced, and famously won events such as Finland's 1000 Lakes rally, the Monte Carlo (three times), the Acropolis, the Circuit of Ireland and many more.

The Mini also attracted celebrity buyers ranging from Peter Sellers and Steve McQueen to Beatles John Lennon and George Harrison – even Enzo Ferrari drove one.

Perhaps the greatest piece of marketing the Mini ever enjoyed, however, was its starring role in the Michael Caine film *The Italian Job* in which a trio of the cars – patriotically painted red, white and blue respectively – were used for an almost-successful heist on a convoy of armoured vehicles transporting gold bullion through Turin.

By the time the film appeared in 1969, however, the Mini was already an automotive legend – and when production finally came to an end in the year 2000, nearly 5.4 million had been produced and sold around the world. Variations on the theme included pick-up, van, estate, convertible and 'face-lifted' Clubman versions, as well as models with extended boot lids and luxurious interiors that were sold under the Riley Elf and Wolseley Hornet names, and the famous, buggy-like 'Moke'.

XLL 27

FASTEN YOUR SEAT

XLL 27

Chevrolet Corvette C1

Production dates: 1953 - 1962
Number built: 69,015
Designer: Harley Earl, Ed Cole
Engine: 235cin/3.8 litre six-cylinder;
265cin/4.3 litre V8; 283/4.6 litre V8; 327cin/5.3 litre V8
Fuel consumption: 10 - 20 mpg
Top speed: 100 - 120 mph

To seafaring types, a corvette is a small warship – but to fans of American automobiles, a Corvette is the first and foremost sports car of the US and a milestone in the country's motoring history.

Thought to have been inspired by the popularity of British two-seaters from marques such as Triumph, Jaguar and Austin-Healey, the Corvette was born from the combined thinking of General Motors 'art and colour studio' chief Harley Earl and Chevrolet chief engineer Ed Cole after they were tasked with creating something new and exciting that would also serve as a low-production experiment in the use of glass fibre for bodywork construction.

In truth, the first Corvette was something of a parts bin special, rather than a true sports car, being fitted with an off-the-shelf, six cylinder 235 cin/ 3.8 litre engine, an uninspiring two-speed Powerglide automatic transmission and a back axle mounted on leaf springs.

All the same, it was given a rapturous reception when the covers came off at the GM Motorama Show at New York's Waldorf Astoria hotel in January 1953. However, of the 5,000-plus that were built for the 1954 model year, just 3,600 were sold.

Despite its racy open-top and generally eye-catching design, the car simply didn't deliver the sportiness it promised and, even when the original model was up-graded with an all-new, 265 cin/4.3 litre V8 engine, the buyers still failed to flock to GM's door.

When the Corvette was re-designed for 1956, however, it was not only better looking but even more powerful and benefited from a three-speed manual gearbox that turned it into a true sports car, with genuine 120 mph performance and the ability to sprint the quarter mile in little more than 14 seconds. For 1956, it was made available with even greater punch thanks to the option of fuel injection that, when bolted to a 283 cin/4.6 litre small block V8 engine, produced an outstanding 283 horsepower.

Luxuries were added, too, including electric windows, a hydraulically operated convertible top and a cutting edge, self-tuning Delco radio. Now the buyers came thick and fast.

Save for the addition of quadruple headlamps, exhaust pipes that exited through the rear bumper, a re-designed dashboard and a few other detail changes – plus an increased range of engine options – the 'Vette' (as it came to be known) remained more or less the same for seven years and established itself as the quintessential American sports car.

When the second generation C2 appeared in 1963, however, it was a different beast altogether...

Not only was it now named the Corvette Stingray, it was an all-round improvement having better handling, better brakes, better suspension and a range of even larger engines – all of which transformed the 'Vette' from a simply pretty, open-top two-seater into a fire-breathing, high-performance muscle car that could more than hold its own on the race track.

But that, as they say, is a whole other story...

1958

Fiat 500

Production dates: 1957 - 1975
Number built: 3,893,294
Designer: Dante Giacosa
Engine: 475/499cc twin-cylinder, air-cooled
Fuel consumption: 40 mpg
Top speed: 55 mph

Anyone who has ever seen a film depicting Rome between the 1950s and the 1970s will have seen a Fiat 500, simply because the streets of every Italian city were swarming with them throughout those decades and beyond.

The tiny, 9ft 9in car was designed as a replacement for Fiat's previous small-sized offering, the Topolino (meaning 'little mouse') by Dante Giacosa, who had earlier created the larger 600D featuring a four-cylinder, water-cooled engine.

As the 500 was intended purely for town and city use, such a complex power unit was not deemed necessary. Instead, it got a twin-cylinder, air-cooled engine that originally displaced just 475cc and was mounted above the rear wheels.

A fully retractable, fabric roof made the most of the Italian summers and there was sufficient space beneath the bonnet to hold the battery, spare wheel and a morning's shopping. Despite the car's diminutive size, its interior could accommodate two average-size adults in the front and offered room for at least one more in the back.

Access was made easier by the use of 'suicide' doors that opened towards the rear of the car, while a decidedly basic equipment level helped to keep the price down and emphasise the 500's practical nature. The sole gauge on the dashboard, for example, was the speedometer, with drivers being left to rely on a 'low fuel' light to remind them when to top-up with 'benzina'.

The 500 proved hugely popular in its original form and the saloon version remained virtually the same throughout the model's 18-year production run, the only significant alterations being an increase in engine capacity to 499cc and a new roof design for 1960's 500D, followed in 1965 by the adoption of conventionally opening doors.

There were, however, extensions to the 500 line thanks to the introduction of a mildly tuned 'Sport' model, the Giardiniera estate version (in which the engine was sited beneath the rear load platform); the Furgoncina panel van; and the 'Jolly' beach car, a conversion carried out by coachbuilder Ghia that turned the 500 into a fully open car with a simple, fabric shade – or 'Surrey' – for a roof.

What few people could have anticipated, however, was the fact that the Fiat 500 might have potential on the race track... Carlo Abarth, founder of tuning house Abarth, designed a big-bore kit that increased cylinder capacity to 593cc and added high compression pistons, a special camshaft, larger carburettor and a free-breathing exhaust system to create the Abarth 595.

The work increased power from the standard Sport model's 22bhp to 30, halved acceleration times and added 25 per cent to the 500's top speed, enabling it to touch almost 80mph. The brakes and suspension were also improved and a more comprehensive dashboard was added – all of which added up to a car for which the term 'giant killer' could have been invented.

In perhaps the ultimate accolade, the Abarth 595 was even chosen as one of the featured cars in the Forza Motorsport racing simulator game series.

FIAT
FIAT
1959
NUOVA 500
2301

Bentley R-Type Continental

Production dates: 1952 - 1955
Number built: 208
Designer: John Blatchley
Engine: 4,566 cc/ 4887cc six-cylinder
Fuel consumption:15 - 20 mpg
Top speed: 120 mph

Seldom has a car carried a more evocative name than the Bentley R-Type Continental – simply reading the words conjures images of beautiful people wafting their way through France at luxurious speed en route to a clifftop villa perched above the sparkling Mediterranean sea.

Surprisingly, however, the car that was once simultaneously the most expensive production model in the world (it cost more than £7,500 at launch in 1952) and the one-time fastest four-seater had its roots in the staid and upright R-Type saloon which, while elegant enough and with decent performance, was hardly a machine to set pulses racing.

The 'Continental', however, substituted the boxy bodywork of the standard steel saloon for a swooping, aerodynamic, two-door silhouette created by the celebrated coachbuilder H.J. Mulliner. Instantly saving 225kg in weight, it was formed throughout from light aluminium, the sporting shape being the result of extensive wind tunnel testing that led to the car being given a sweeping, finned rear end to create stability enhancing downforce.

Under the vast bonnet nestled the same, basic 4.5 litre engine (later enlarged to 4.9 litres) used in the R-Type Saloon, but with a modified carburettor, a higher compression ratio and more efficient exhaust and induction systems. The final gear ratios, meanwhile, were increased to provide the type of loping, high-speed performance that would make continent crossing an effortless pleasure.

The result, concluded a lyrical *Autocar* journalist, was that 'The Bentley is a modern magic carpet which annihilates great distances and delivers the occupants well-nigh as fresh as when they started.'

Of the 207 R-Type Continentals produced, however, not all were the same. While many were bodied by H.J. Mulliner in the fastback coupé form previously described, other cars were completed in small batches with similar-but-different 'looks' created by London coachbuilder Park Ward, Graber of Switzerland, Pininfarina of Italy and Marius Franay of Paris.

Such is the importance and rarity of the model that the whereabouts of most surviving examples are known – although a 'lost' one does occasionally re-surface, as in the case of a 1953 model that appeared at auction in California in 2016.

Shortly before the sale, the white, entirely original car had been discovered parked in a garage where it is believed to have stood since the late 1970s. Subsequent research revealed it to have been ordered new by none other than James Bond author Ian Fleming.

Fleming had bought the car on behalf of his close friend Ivar Bryce, the man who inspired him to build his famous home 'Goldeneye' in Jamaica and whose surname appears in the novels *Dr No* and *Live and Let Die*.

So perhaps it is no coincidence that, in the 1961 Bond book *Thunderball*, Fleming puts 007 in a Bentley Continental – albeit one with a bespoke, convertible, two-seater body that, according to the author, made it 'the most selfish car in England.'

He really should have stuck with Mulliner's decidedly generous original...

Citroën DS19

Citroën DS 19
Production dates: 1955 - 1975
Number built: 1,445,960
Designer: Flaminio Bertoni, André Lefèbvre
Engine: 1,911cc, 1,985cc four-cylinder
Fuel consumption: 20 - 30 mpg
Top speed: 100 - 110 mph

If you've ever wondered what a car designed by an Italian sculptor and a French aeronautical engineer might look like, cast an eye over Citroën's DS19. Still considered radical almost 70 years after its launch at the Paris motor show in 1955, the much-loved DS was the result of a joint effort between Flaminio Bertoni (the sculptor) and André Lefèbvre (the aero engineer) who were detailed to create a replacement for the celebrated Traction Avant that, while once equally innovative, had by then been around since 1937.

When the covers came off the DS, the public reaction was one of shock and awe. Never before had such a space-age design been created by a European manufacturer, and never before had such advanced engineering featured on a car intended for mass production.

It was, for example, the first regular road car to feature power disc brakes – and they were operated by a tiny, floor-mounted button (playfully known as a 'mushroom') that responded instantly to the very slightest touch of the foot.

The car also offered a remarkable level of comfort and handling thanks to its hydro-pneumatic suspension, which not only enabled the ride height to be raised or lowered according to road conditions but allowed a wheel to be changed without recourse to a conventional jack. The power-assisted steering, meanwhile, could be operated with the pressure of a single finger, and the car's aerodynamic shape made for impressive fuel economy and unusually low noise levels.

Within 15 minutes of the DS being unveiled in Paris, Citroën had taken a remarkable 743 deposits – a number that rose to 80,000 by the time the 10-day motor show came to an end. It was a sales record that stood for more than 60 years before being overtaken in 2016 when the order books opened for Tesla's Model 3.

If the DS had a fault, however, it lay with its somewhat sluggish performance. Essentially, the car was simply too big for the sub 2-litre engines that were fitted to early models in order to avoid the high taxation applied to larger capacity automobiles – and even though the updated DS 20, 21 and 23 had engines of up to 2.4 litres, speed was never the car's forte.

What it did become renowned for, however, was reliability. So long as the complex, high-pressure hydraulic system was correctly maintained (and kept topped-up with the required special fluid) a DS was as dependable as the day was long, with especially prepared examples proving their worth in gruelling long distance rallies.

It is even said that a DS saved the life of President Charles de Gaulle after the one he was travelling in was sprayed with bullets during an assassination attempt. With punctured tyres, most 'ordinary' cars would have been forced to grind to a halt, but the sophisticated, self-levelling suspension system on the DS enabled it to be driven at speed to a place of safety.

Variations on the model included the additionally luxurious 'Pallas' that became a popular ministerial car; the 'Safari' estate

version which had a vast carrying capacity and was supplied with a factory-fitted roof rack; and the seven-seater 'Familiale' which offered an additional second bench. Many DS estates were also turned into commercial vehicles, such as ambulances and television camera cars.

The DS variant that is now considered the most valuable of all, however, is the limited production 'Decapotable' that was created, with Citroën's blessing, by the French coachbuilder Henri Chapron who based the elegant, open model on a strengthened estate car chassis.

Just 1,365 official Citroën conversions were produced, with Chapron completing a further 389 of his own. The best now sell for £100,000 - 150,000.

BO·562·HJ
3516 WS 50
2

Le Monde de la DS
DS 60e anniversaire
AM-51-53

1960s

Mini Moke

Production dates: 1964 - 1968 (original UK-built models)
Number built: 14,518
Designer: Alec Issigonis
Engine: 850cc, 998cc, 1098cc and 1275cc, four cylinder
Fuel consumption - 40 mpg
Top speed: 70 - 80 mph

'Not fit for purpose' was the conclusion of the British Army's esteemed procurement officers following evaluation of condename 'Buckboard', a bare-bones utility vehicle conceived in 1959 by Mini inventor Alec Issigonis and his colleague John Sheppard.

The Buckboard was designed to be robust enough to withstand a parachute drop, spacious enough to carry four burly soldiers and light enough to be picked up by them when the going got tough. With fold-flat windscreens and angular wheel arches, Buckboards could even be stacked on top of one another – but from a military point of view, the Mini-based vehicle proved next to useless due to its low power, low ground clearance and lack of four-wheel-drive.

Yet its makers BMC (the British Motor Corporation) refused to be daunted by the Army's rejection and decided to market the no-frills project for civilian use. Re-named the Mini 'Moke' after a colloquial word for donkey, it went on sale in 1964, ostensibly as a lightweight farm vehicle which didn't attract purchase tax. Initially priced at £405, it was utilitarian in the extreme with only one solid metal seat, one windscreen wiper and one paint option: spruce green. Luxuries such as passenger seats and windscreen washers were available as optional extras.

Between 1964 and 1968, BMC's Longbridge plant churned-out more than 14,000 Mokes, around 90 per cent of which were shipped abroad for use in warmer climes where the doorless, roofless cars became popular as island runabouts, beach buggies, taxis and low-cost rentals. Mokes were subsequently made in Australia until 1981 and Portugal from 1980 to 1993, with production finally ending after around 50,000 had been built and sold.

By then, the Moke had well and truly achieved cult status. Having been quickly adopted as a groovy vehicle in which to make the transition from the '60s to the '70s, it had also found favour among the international jet set as a cute riviera runabout, appeared in the TV series *The Prisoner* as well as several James Bond movies, and demonstrated its ability to transcend social barriers by selling to everyone from sheep farmers to tycoons such as Aristotle Onassis and the Aga Khan.

Numerous variations on the theme were also created, with Mokes being offered in an array of different colours, with engines of 998cc, 1098cc and 1275cc. There were a range of jaunty trim options that included roofs and seats made from multi-coloured vinyls with names such as 'Orange Bali' and 'Op-pop Verve'. Perhaps the strangest of all Mokes, however, were the handful which were converted for use as inspection vehicles to run on the tracks of the Tasmanian and Australian railways.

Until relatively recently, a decent Moke could still be picked-up for as little as £1,500 – but soaring demand from buyers enamoured of their retro-chic simplicity has seen prices for the best examples exceed the £20,000 mark, with many being bought as holiday home runabouts for cruising to the beach with the top down and a full complement of sun-kissed passengers.

For this, of course, they are entirely 'fit for purpose'.

MOKE

AUSTIN
GCP 85E

MG MGB

Production dates: 1962 - 1980
Number built: 514,834
Designer:
Engine: 1798cc, four cylinder
Fuel consumption - 30 mpg
Top speed: 109 mph

The year 1962 was quite a special one for cars. It produced the Ferrari GTO, the Shelby Cobra, the Lotus Elan and the rather more pedestrian Triumph Spitfire – but, perhaps best of all, it produced the MGB.

The beloved B captured the very essence of the swinging sixties with its simple style, elegant performance and throaty exhaust note – it could almost have been built for cruising to Carnaby Street. In reality, it was designed as the replacement for the ageing MGA and was the British marque's first car to feature monocoque construction rather than having its bodywork bolted to a separate chassis.

This made it more solid and gave it the sure-footed handling and entirely modern feel that proved the key to its impressive, 18-year production span during which more than half a million rolled-off the line at the MG works in Abingdon, Oxfordshire.

Indeed, looking at a B today, it seems difficult to believe that it was created half a century ago – which partly explains why it is widely regarded as the world's most popular classic sports car and continues to be a familiar sight on modern roads.

Opinion is, however, divided over which is the best B of all. Purists favour the original roadster that was produced from 1962 to 1967 with its dashboard of simple toggle switches, its pull-handle doors and proper leather seats; others appreciate the practicality of the GT coupé that was introduced in 1965, with its hard roof, hatchback door and small 'occasional' rear seat which, by modern safety standards, might be considered quite lethal despite seeming entirely adequate for children and adults alike in more carefree days.

The cars with the standard 1800cc engines were the most ubiquitous, although there was also the rare, factory-built BGT V8 made in 2,591 examples from 1973–1976, the aftermarket V8 conversions built by engineer Ken Costello and even the flawed MGC, an unwieldy marriage of the B's roadster or GT body with a six-cylinder, 2.9 litre engine.

Sadly, however, the B didn't exactly get better with the passing years. With America being its main export market, it began to suffer from safety and emissions legislation which saw its power output significantly reduced and, worst of all, resulted in its elegant chrome bumpers being substituted for hefty black rubber items which necessitated an ungainly one-inch hike in ride height.

By the late 1970s, sports cars had temporarily lost their charm, the B was showing its age and sales had slowed to a trickle. In a bid to offload the last 1,000, MG produced 500 roadsters and 500 GTs in 'limited edition' livery of gold and silver respectively prior to the Abingdon factory's doors being closed for the final time.

Essentially, the B became just another old motor – until the classic car bubble that began to inflate in the late 1980s came to its rescue. Suddenly, MGBs were being restored left, right and centre (some more badly than others) and an extensive network of parts suppliers and makers grew-up around the world, so saving numerous cars from the scrap heap.

Nowadays, many such cars have been restored again, often to a far better standard, and the B is now the most ubiquitous classic sports car on the market – which means buyers are at liberty to shop around until they find the perfect example.

Lamborghini Miura

Production dates: 1966 - 1973
Number built: 746
Designer: Marcello Gandini for Bertone
Engine: V12, 3929cc. 350 - 380 bhp
Fuel consumption - 12 mpg
Top speed: 170 mph plus

The curvaceous Lamborghini Miura found fame in the opening sequence of the Michael Caine movie *The Italian Job*, during which a crimson example is seen snaking along an Alpine pass on the Italian-Swiss border to the accompaniment of singer Matt Monro crooning 'On Days Like These'. The driver, actor Rossano Brazzi, is concentrating on guiding the Miura swiftly between the switchbacks at a healthy pace – until he enters a tunnel and ploughs head-on into a Mafia bulldozer that tips the car and driver into an adjacent gorge.

Rather happier is the story of how the Miura came to be in the first place. It is said to have been designed by Lamborghini engineers aged in their early 20s during their spare time, because boss Ferruccio Lamborghini was more interested in grand touring cars than racers for the street – which is exactly what the Miura became with its 172mph top speed, courtesy of a 12-cylinder, four-litre engine crammed in behind the two-seater cockpit.

The layout offered sublime handling but the car's brutal power, over-light front end, cacophonous engine noise and a gear change that has been described as 'like trying to pull Excalibur from its stone' ensured that naming the Miura after a fighting bull was entirely appropriate.

Nevertheless, its 'wow' factor ensured that it was eagerly received as the plaything of the rich and famous, attracting buyers such as Miles Davis, Frank Sinatra and the Shah of Iran. Its already stand-out looks, meanwhile, were enhanced by the availability of wild, of-the-era paint options, such as lime green, acid orange and vibrant yellow.

During its relatively short production run, the Miura was upgraded from the original P400 model to the P400S and then to the P400SV, the most powerful of all the standard variants.

There was also a unique convertible and, in 1970, a one-off car called the Jota was developed for racing, which sold to a private buyer after extensive testing – only to be crashed and burnt out on the unopened Brescia ring road while it was being delivered.

It quickly became a Lamborghini legend, prompting calls from customers for the factory to make road-going Jotas. The firm then built five SVJs (SVs with Jota upgrades), the most famous of which was delivered to the Shah in St Moritz.

It ended up back at Tehran's Royal Palace – allegedly under armed guard – until the Iranian Revolution of 1979, when it went to Dubai before being bought at auction in 1997 by Hollywood star Nicolas Cage for $500,000. It was then acquired in 2004 by the Iranian enthusiast Reza Rashidian, who kept it for around four years before selling it privately for a record sum, rumoured by enthusiasts to have been 'well into seven figures'.

Lamborghini
ORLANDO

JAEGER
ACQUA
AMPERES

Lamborghini
Miura

bertone

Jaguar E-Type

Production dates: 1961 - 1975
Number built: 72,515 (road cars only)
Designer: Malcolm Sayer
Engine: 3.8 litre, 4.2 litre six cylinder; 5.3 litre V12
Fuel consumption: 15 - 20 mpg
Top speed: 150 mph

When talk turns to the cars of the swinging sixties, you can bet your string-backed driving gloves that it won't belong before Jaguar's E-Type becomes the focus of attention. Created by former aircraft designer Malcolm Sayer, the design was first unveiled outside the Restaurant du Parc des Eaux Vives during the Geneva Salon at 4.30pm on March 15, 1961.

Its radical appearance and promise of being 'the fastest production car in the world' caused near hysteria and resulted in 500 orders being placed before the show had ended.

Beneath its famously long bonnet lurked a six-cylinder, 3.8 litre, 265 horsepower engine that gave this most beautiful of felines a top speed of 150mph – yet, at £2,098 for the roadster and £2,197 for the fixed-head coupé, it cost less than half the price of a comparable Ferrari or Aston Martin.

During its 14-year production run, the E-Type evolved to feature first a 4.2 litre engine and, ultimately, Jaguar's 5.3 litre V12. It was offered with manual or automatic transmission and, in final 'Series 3' form, the fixed-head car was made available only as a more family friendly two-plus-two model.

More than 72,000 E-Types were built, with around 12,000 being sold in Britain and the majority going to the USA. Celebrated owners included Frank Sinatra, George Harrison, Britt Ekland, Peter Sellers and Sir Jackie Stewart. These days, the most sought after model remains the Series 1 'flat floor' roadster – with original, 1961 examples now fetching up to £200,000.

But, although production of the original model officially ceased in 1975, Jaguar's modern day 'Classic' division recently revived it in two very special – and very different – forms.

The first came about in 2014 when it was announced that the firm would complete the 'Lightweight E-Type' project started in 1963 which resulted in the creation of a series of highly focused racing versions of the standard car. Officially called the Special GT E-Type, they featured all-aluminium bodies and engine blocks, stripped-out interiors and numerous other weight-saving deletions.

Only twelve of the intended eighteen cars were made, however, leaving the remaining half-dozen allocated chassis numbers on file. And it is those that were used by Jaguar to build the six 'missing' Lightweights which sold to specially selected Jaguar clients for a price rumoured to have been around £1.2 million apiece.

Even more surprising, however, was the 2017 news that Jaguar had created an all-electric version of the '60s automotive icon – and it is claimed to be smoother, quieter, lighter and considerably less expensive to run than the original, while remaining every bit as good looking.

The car, dubbed 'E-Type Zero,' is based on a 1968 Roadster that has been fitted with a bespoke, state-of-the-art electric powertrain, modified instrumentation and energy-saving LED headlamps. The conversion has been carried out in such a way that an original engine can be re-installed in order to maintain authenticity.

The aim, says Jaguar, is to 'future-proof' classic car ownership in a world that is becoming increasingly intolerant of fossil fuel emissions and increasingly open to accepting alternative forms of propulsion. And the fact that the pre-V12 E-Types were fitted with the same, six-cylinder engine used in other classic Jaguars such as the XK120, MK II and XJ means that the electric powertrain can be used to convert several different models...

MAR
ARIZONA 73
VLA-977

Shelby Cobra

Production dates: 1962 - 1968
Number built: 1,003
Designer: Carroll Shelby
Engine: 260 cin (4.3 litre) 289 cin (4.7 litre) or 427 cin (7 litre) V8
Fuel consumption - 15 mpg
Top speed: 120 - 165 mph

For those unfamiliar with the name of Carroll Shelby, he was a successful, Le Mans-winning Texan racing driver who had to give up competing in 1959 at the age of 36 due to a long-standing heart problem.

Although he was given only a short time to live (he actually died more than 50 years later aged 89) he set up a performance driving school and founded Shelby American which, in 1962, began importing British-built AC Ace sports cars into the US and fitting them with Ford V8 engines in place of the less powerful units they were originally supplied with.

The first production Cobras used 4.3 litre engines and were upgraded with better disc brakes, improved suspension and a tougher back axle than the standard AC Ace in order to cope with the huge power hike from around 120 bhp in the normal, Bristol-engined AC Ace to a heady 240 bhp with the Ford V8 installed.

The result was so 'venomous' that the new, Anglo-American hybrid was named the Shelby Cobra – and it proved to be hugely successful both as a high-performance street machine and as a racing car.

Although the prototype Cobra was assembled at AC's factory in Thames Ditton, Surrey, the model was really created for the American market. As a result, production versions began their lives in the UK as painted and trimmed rolling chassis which were then shipped to Los Angeles where the engines (which were supplied by Ford as part of an official deal) were fitted along with suitably robust gearboxes.

So great was the demand for the Cobra that, by early 1963, AC was forced to drop production of its other models. The more Cobras that were built, the better they became, as the cars' ancillaries were refined to make the most of the huge horsepower. This became even greater as first a 4.7 litre, 270 horsepower engine was added to the range before the ultimate Cobra arrived in 1965 in the form of the MK III 427 'big block'.

Ford's fire-breathing, 427 cubic inch (or seven litre) powerplant instantly made the Cobra the most fearsome sports car on the market – and one which became famed for being able to lay-down quarter-mile long strips of rubber as its fat tyres struggled to cope with the engine's prodigious output.

Although production of the Shelby Cobra lasted little more than 5 years with only around 1,000 original examples being built, its fame was such that it became one of the most imitated of all car designs with clones, kits, replicas and 'tribute' models being produced by manufacturers around the world.

In 1996, however, Shelby American returned to building Cobras in Los Angeles and a new one can be bought today for between $100,000 and $500,000 depending on the specification, finish and whether or not the body is built from aluminium or glass fibre.

In either case, it's cheap compared with the $13.8 million that chassis number CSX2000 realised at auction in 2016. Mind you, it was the very first Cobra to have been built.

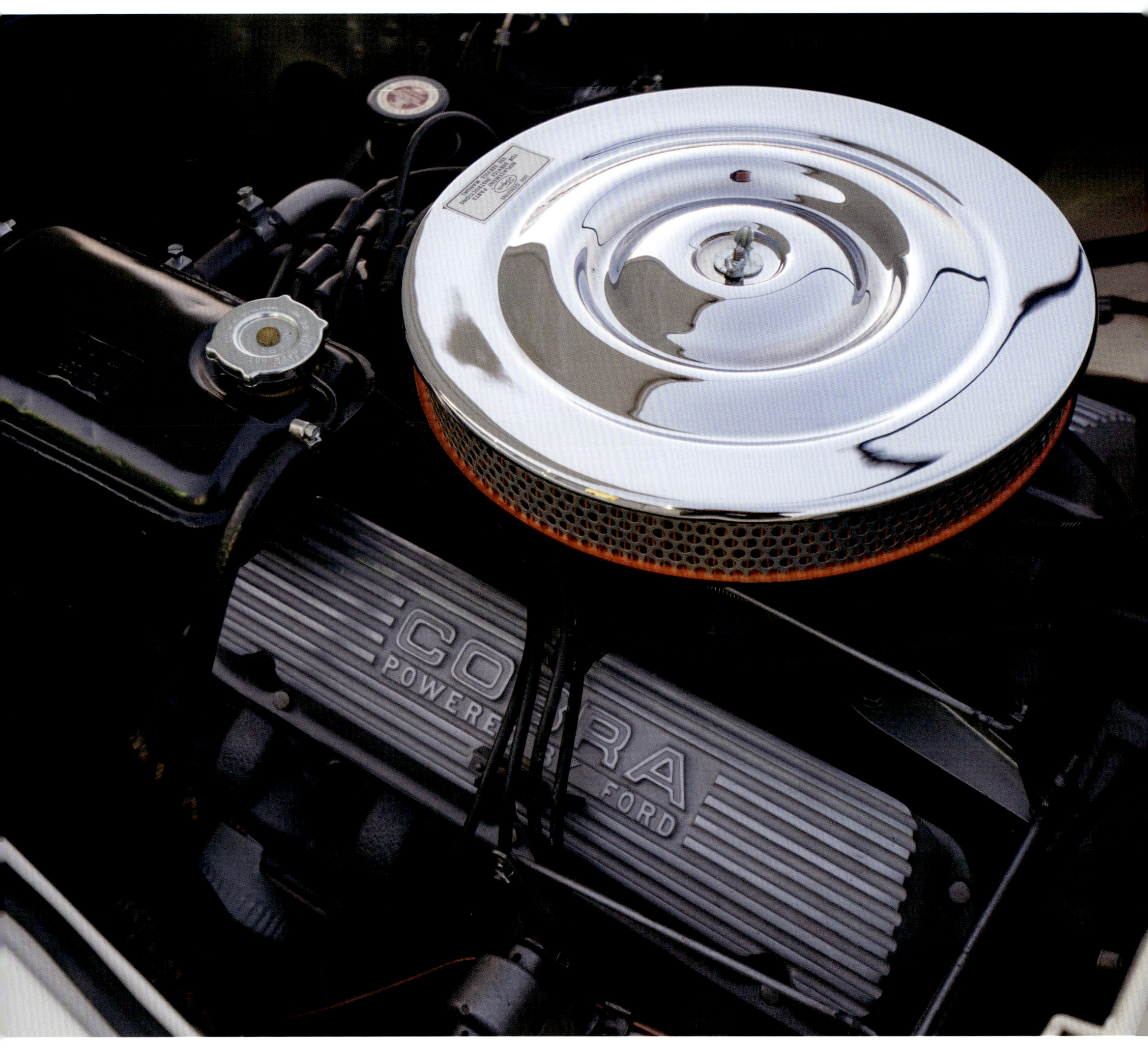
FORD

Ferrari 250 GTO

Production dates: 1962 - 1964
Number built: 39
Designer: Giotto Bizzarrini
Engine: Three-litre and four-litre, V12
Fuel consumption: 8 - 15 mpg
Top speed: 174 mph

Even those with no more than a passing interest in old cars will probably have heard of the legendary Ferrari 250 'GTO', if only because examples have, on several occasions, held the record for being the most expensive cars to have sold at auction.

The story of the GTO – which stands for Gran Turismo Omologato – begins with Enzo Ferrari's determination to further his marque's success in GT racing, as established by models such as the earlier 250GT with the creation of a car that could show a clean pair of heels to challengers such as Aston Martin, Porsche, Shelby and Jaguar.

Giotto Bizzarrini undertook the initial engineering design, with the rear suspension being worked on by Mauro Forghieri and the bodywork being entrusted to coachbuilder Scaglietti.

The 'Omologato' in the name referred to the FIA homologation rules that required cars competing in Group Three of the GT championship to have been among a minimum of 100 produced for road use. But, since Ferrari had no intention of building 100 GTOs, he is said to have 'jumped' chassis numbers to give the impression that many more cars existed than actually did.

In reality, a mere 39 were ever completed, 36 with three-litre engines (the '250' refers to the cubic capacity of each of the engines 12, tiny cylinders) and three cars with four-litre engines. Of these, 33 had 'series one' bodywork, three had 'series two' bodywork and three were 'specials'.

Inside, the GTO was very much a 'working office' with blue cloth bucket seats bolted to a bare alloy floor, a metal 'crackle finish' dashboard and height adjustable brake and clutch pedals. There was no headlining or carpet, a quilted shroud covered the gearbox and rear windows were made from plastic. The two-speed windscreen wipers, meanwhile, were powered by a British Lucas electric motor and a minimal parcel shelf occupied the void in the rear in order to comply with FIA regulations requiring 'luggage space'.

When it became available in 1962, the car's gorgeous looks and 174mph top speed quickly had potential buyers forming a disorderly queue – but Ferrari and his American importer, Luigi Chinetti, chose owners carefully in order to ensure that the GTOs would end up only in the hands of talented and experienced racing drivers.

As a result, the car achieved second place in its debut race at the 12 Hours of Sebring in the hands of American F1 world champion Phil Hill and Belgian co-driver Olivier Gendebien, after which the wins just kept coming, with drivers such as Graham Hill, John Surtees, Roy Salvadori and Stirling Moss campaigning GTOs to victory at major events around the world and helping Ferrari to consecutive wins in the International GT Championship in 1962, '63 and '64.

As well as being a remarkable performer on the track, the GTO was also easy and forgiving to drive on the road. The day after Belgians Jean Blaton and Gerald Langlois van Ophem won the GT category at the Le Mans

24 Hours in 1963, for example, they jumped back into their car, drove to Paris for a party and then continued home to Brussells.

By the mid '60s, however, the 250 GTO had become just another old racer put out to pasture and examples could be bought for less than a quarter of their original $18,500 sale price, with one being sold at auction in 1969 for just $2,500. Pink Floyd drummer Nick Mason, meanwhile, claims to have paid £35,000 for his GTO in 1977 – an amount that he considered, at the time, to have been 'stupid'.

The classic car boom of the 1980s saw prices rocket, however, with a 1962 car being hammered down for £6.4 million in May 1990 (although the sale ultimately fell through).

Since then prices have risen rapidly, to the point that the current auction record for a GTO (and for any car) stands at $38.1m (£22.8m), a price achieved by Bonhams in 2014.

It is rumoured, however, that another GTO changed hands for as much as $50 million in a private deal...

F.VIOLATI · S.VIOLATI

Ford Mustang

Production dates: 1964 - 1973 (first generation)
Number built: 2.9 million
Designer: Joe Oros
Engine: 200 cin (3.2 litre) six cylinder; 289 cin (4.7 litre) V8; 302 cin (4.0 litre); 351 cin (5.7 litre) V8; 390 cin (6.3 litre) V8; 427 cin (7 litre) V8; 428 cin V8
Fuel consumption: 10 - 25 mpg
Top speed: 100 - 140 mph

Market research is often described as a load of old baloney – but the crystal ball used by the team hired to predict what young and trendy types with money in their pockets might want to drive in the mid 1960s proved to be spot-on. And the answer was Ford's magical Mustang.

The number crunchers had discovered that the post-war baby boom would see the amount of people in the 15 to 29 age group soar by 40 per cent during the 1960s with the result that, for the first time in history, the majority of America's population would be below the age of 25 – and with the economy growing and enjoyment well and truly on the agenda, many of them would have money burning holes in their pockets.

In late 1960, Lido (or 'Lee' as he liked to be called) Iacocca had become head of Ford Division at the young age of 36. Recognising the forthcoming shift in the market, he called for the creation of a new, two-door car that was not a 'sports car' per se but had a sporting image. It was to follow the trend recently established by the general Motors Monza coupé for a smaller-scale American car and was to be made available with a vast range of options in order to make it affordable to the greatest number of buyers and types of driver.

The first Mustang prototype had a V4 engine mounted in the middle and only two seats – a combination that wowed those who saw it but wasn't what Iacocca wanted. And neither were the numerous other prototypes with a multitude of potential model names that poured from the Ford drawing board before, $65 million of development money later, the Mustang proper was born.

Launched in April 1964 with a $10m promotional campaign that saw it on the covers of both *Newsweek* and *Time* magazines and revealed it to 30 million Americans through prime time TV commercials, the Mustang went on sale at a starting price of $2,368. During the first weekend it was available, an estimated four million people flocked to Ford dealerships around the country see one in the flesh.

A remarkable 100,000 were sold in the first four months, with annual sales peaking in 1966 when Ford shifted 540,802. Few buyers bought the most basic version, however, with most adding at least $600 worth of options, ranging from whitewall tyres ($33.90) to vinyl roofs ($75.80).

But there was much more to be had than that because Mustangs were soon available not only in the original 'notchback' form but in convertible and fastback body styles, too. Up to twenty colour options were offered along with six-cylinder or V8 engines of various capacities, manual or automatic gearboxes and drum or disc brakes. Interiors could be specified with various levels of trim, instrumentation and accessories.

It all helped the now legendary 'Pony Car' to become a smash hit with everyone from college students to middle-class mothers and, after high-performance Mustangs had shown their mettle in competition and Steve McQueen had driven the wheels off one in the cult car chase movie *Bullitt*, there was barely a country in the world where the name didn't resonate.

As the years went by, however, the Mustang gradually lost its character, first becoming larger, then slower, then smaller and then, well, just rather mediocre until the fifth generation model was introduced in 2005 – sporting a shape heavily inspired by the original.

Which, as everyone knows, is always the best...

FORD

ARIZONA
BOSS429
GOODYEAR
POLYGLAS GT

28
POLYGLAS GT
GOODYEAR

Aston Martin DB5

Production dates: 1963 - 1965
Number built:1,025
Designer: Tadek Marek (engine) Touring of Milan (body)
Engine: Four litre, six-cylinder
Fuel consumption: 15 - 20 mpg
Top speed: 145 mph

The title of 'world's most famous car' could fairly be attributed to Aston Martin's fabled DB5, the sight of which has come to be recognised the world over thanks to the model being James Bond's choice in no fewer than eight movies (at time of writing) since making its screen debut with the release of *Goldfinger* in September 1964.

By then, the DB5 was already half way through its model life, having been launched exactly a year earlier as a replacement for the DB4 that arrived in 1958 to rapturous applause thanks to its 140mph performance, gorgeous Carrozzeria Touring 'superleggera' bodywork and richly trimmed interior.

During the first years of production the DB4 was plagued with mechanical problems which, although mostly ironed-out by the time the DB5 came along, meant the new car benefited from a fresh and reliable all-aluminium engine that produced a healthy 282 horsepower and gave the car better acceleration and a top speed of 145mph.

The DB4's gearbox problems were also resolved on the DB5 by a change to a tough, five-speed unit built by the German manufacturer ZF, the whole package resulting in 1,025 being built and sold in two years compared with the five years it took to sell 1,185 examples of the '4'.

Among those 1,025 DB5s there were just 65 high-performance Vantage versions featuring more racy camshafts and triple Weber carburettors (in place of the three, standard SUs), boosting the engine's output to 315 horsepower. There were also 123 convertibles built (12 with the Vantage engine) and even a dozen or so 'shooting brake' conversions following the creation of an initial example for Aston Martin's then owner David Brown, a keen game shot who wanted a DB5 in which he could transport his dogs and guns.

As good a car as the DB5 was (and is), however, there is no denying that its fame is mainly attributable to the connection with Bond that came about after Aston Martin agreed to loan two cars to Eon productions for film use during the making of *Goldfinger*.

Of those, one was sold as a 'used car' in the late 1960s only to end up being stolen from its storage hangar in 1997 never to be seen again; the other, having appeared in both *Goldfinger* and *Thunderball* carrying the famous registration mark FMP 7B and having been used to publicise the films around the world, was bought from the factory in 1969 by an American radio station owner called Jerry Lee.

Lee displayed the car at his home as the highlight of a private collection of Bond memorabilia until deciding to part with it through auction house RM Sotheby's in October 2010.

Remarkably, the car was offered complete with its celebrated movie gadgets such as switches for smoke screen and oil slick making, nail spreading and number plate revolving; a pop-up, boot-mounted steel bullet shield; wing-mounted machine guns; telescopic bumper rams; tyre slashers; ejection seat; door-mounted telephone and radio receiver.

Inevitably the sale of the car attracted interest from around the world, provoking a frenzied bidding battle that resulted in its final sale for £2.9 million to US businessman Harry Yeaggy.

This was rather more than the $12,000 Lee had paid Aston Martin for it 40 years earlier...

JB007

FMP 7B

1970s

Range Rover 'Classic'

Production dates: 1970 - 1995
Number built: 325,490
Designer: Charles Spencer King
Engine: 3,500cc V8 petrol, 3,900cc V8 petrol, 4,200cc V8 petrol; 2.4 litre and 2.5 litre diesel
Fuel consumption: 15 - 30 mpg
Top speed: 90 - 110 mph

Some people believe Charles Spencer King has a lot to answer for: As the designer of the original Range Rover, it could be said that he caused the boom in what are nowadays referred to as 'sports utility vehicles', those *bêtes noires* of the environmental brigade that are variously charged with destroying the planet, riding rough-shod over cyclists and, worst of all, causing terrible parking problems at the school gates.

Yet in other circles, King's work is regarded as a stroke of genius and now examples of his inspired creation, which brilliantly combined the off-road capabilities of a Land Rover with the comfort of a luxury saloon, have achieved classic status in the original shape that lasted from the official unveiling in June 1970 until 1995.

As far back as the 1950s Rover was toying with the idea of making a go-anywhere vehicle and produced 23 prototype 'Road Rovers' between 1951 and 1959, but didn't believe there was a market for them until the emergence in 1960s America of four-wheel-drive leisure vehicles caused King to formulate the initial specification for the Range Rover prototype which was so secret that it was given the code-name 'Velar' – the Latin word for to hide or to conceal.

Plans for an African launch were abandoned in favour of the cheaper, more British option of using an old Cornish tin mine and, on June 17, 1970, the early examples were tested by the press and received a rapturous response – so much so that by the time the first cars went on sale on September 1 for £1,998, deals had already been done to pass them on for a profit to eager buyers further down the waiting list.

Although around 40 Velars were built, the Range Rover name was used from the outset on production models which were targeted towards wealthy, successful types who also lived life to the full. Typical advertisements showed Range Rovers wafting along motorways pulling speedboats or parked-up at the gliding club, usually in the care of well-groomed men dressed in the latest synthetic fabrics and occasionally being fawned over by pretty girls in flared trousers.

The Range Rover's superb off-road ability and genuine ruggedness was also demonstrated by its participation in events such as the British Trans Americas expedition of 1971–1972, in which Major (now Colonel) John Blashford-Snell and a crew from the 17th/21st Lancers covered 18,000 miles of the Pan-American Highway – 250 miles of which crossed the infamous Darien Gap, a roadless, swamp-covered jungle which took the team three months to conquer.

By the time the 1990s arrived, however, the original Range Rover's boxy styling, wallowing, boat-like ride, greedy appetite for fuel and sometimes questionable reliability had seen the value of all but the very best examples drop to three figures, with many being scrapped, irreparably modified or cannibalised for parts.

But now the design is again recognised for its brilliance and so-called 'Classic' Range Rovers have become highly collectable. Many enthusiasts favour the two-door body for its simplicity and no-nonsense interior, which featured plastic seats and rubber mats designed to be cleaned by hosepipe – but the less austere trim of later years and the four-door body style that arrived in 1981 also has its followers.

Particularly sought after is the rare, limited edition 'CSK' version that was made in 1991 to honour Charles Spencer King. All 200 were finished in gleaming black and combined the original, two-door body style with the later, 3.9 litre, fuel injection engine, upgraded brakes and suspension and a special interior.

The best can now command up to £100,000.

Typical advertisements showed Range Rovers wafting along motorways pulling speedboats or parked-up at the gliding club.

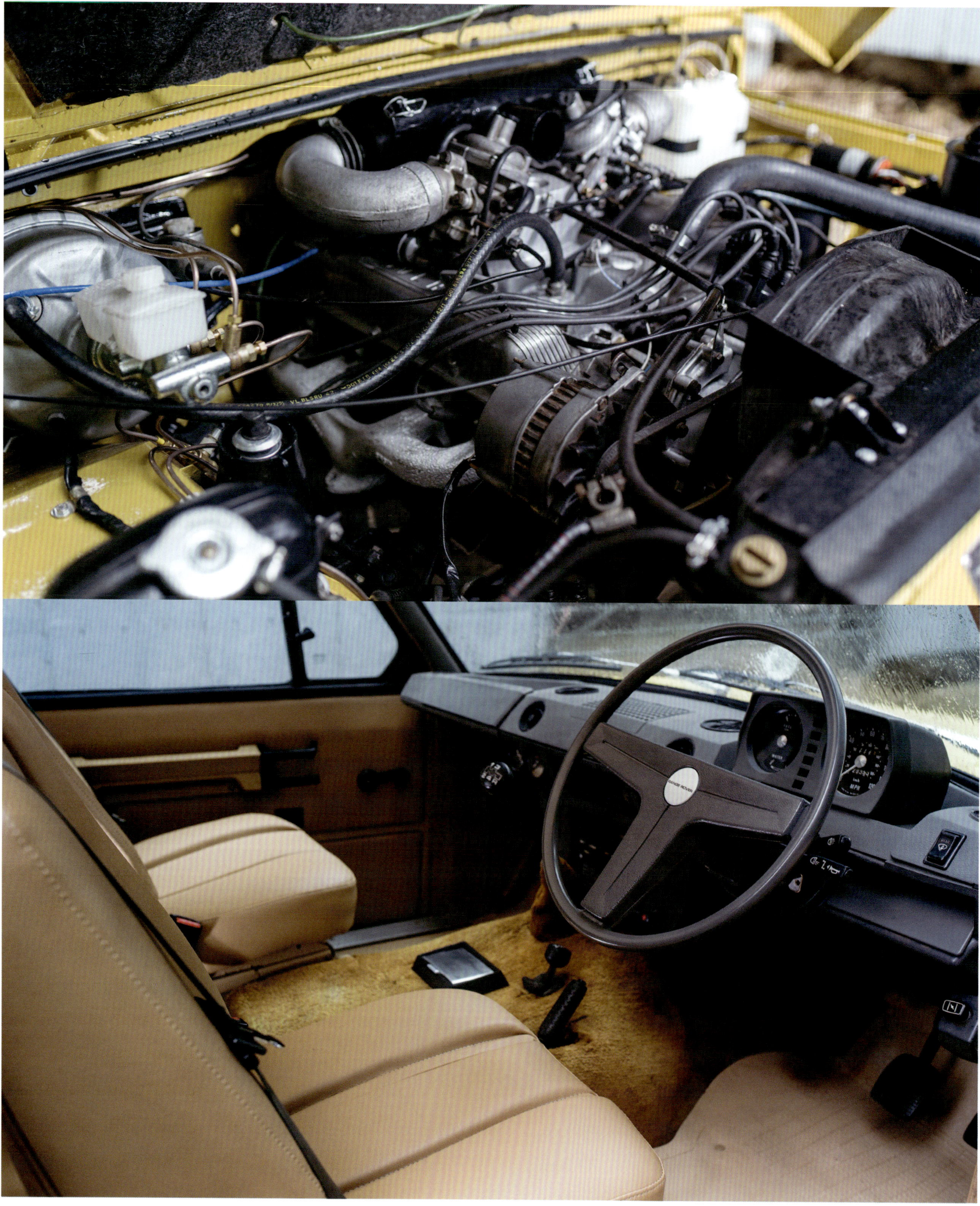

RANGE ROVER

RANGE ROVER

Iso Grifo Series II

Production dates: 1970 - 1973
Number built: 78 (Series II)
Designer: Giotto Bizzarrini
Engine: 427 cin (7 litre) or 454 cin (7.4 litre) V8
Fuel consumption: 15 - 18 mpg
Top speed: 170 mph

Considering that some still regard it as a bit of a mongrel, Italy's Iso Grifo has a pretty impressive pedigree. Its sleek, grand-tourer bodywork was penned by Giorgetto Giugiaro (whose CV also includes the Lotus Esprit and the Volkswagen Golf); its mechanicals were designed by Giotto Bizzarrini (who was responsible for Ferrari's celebrated 250 GTO, found on page 152); and its powerplant came from the Chevrolet Corvette (see page 106).

The brainchild of Iso founder Renzo Rivolta (whose industrialist forebears made a fortune from products as diverse as bubble cars and refrigerators), the sporting two-seater was launched in 1965 to be sold alongside the two-plus-two Iso Rivolta.

The Grifo, named after the griffin, the mythical king of beasts, was intended to provide serious competition to the likes of Ferrari and Maserati by combining the beauty and style for which Italian GT cars were renowned with the strength and reliability for which they were not – hence the use of tough American gearboxes and V8 engines which were shipped complete from the US to Italy before being stripped down, blueprinted and re-assembled to ensure optimum performance.

The first models used 'small block', 5.4-litre Corvette powerplants which, thanks to the Grifo weighing less than 1,000kg, gave a top speed of around 170mph – instantly making it the fastest road car of the day.

Just 413 Grifos are believed to have been built during the nine-year production run, each of which was assembled by hand from the ground up in Series I, Series II and IR-8 versions, the latter two featuring larger-capacity engines of up to 7.4 litres and a restyled front end that partially hid the car's headlamps.

Although the Series I models are highly sought after for their clean lines, it is the Series II versions introduced in 1970 that represent the pinnacle of Grifo production in terms of performance and development, with the rarest of the rare being the 'targa' version of the car (featuring a lift-out roof section), a mere four examples of which were built.

A large number of Grifos were sold to Germany, where their pace made them popular on the autobahns; a significant quantity went to the US; and a mere 32 right-hand-drive models were imported to the UK before the oil crisis of 1973 caused a dramatic fall in demand for such large-engined gas guzzlers, leading to the permanent closure of 'Iso Autoveicoli' the following year.

Had that not happened, many believe Iso would have gone on to become more widely recognised as a maker of truly great cars – a theory evinced by the fact that a large proportion of Grifos built still survive, despite their curvaceous steel bodywork being prone to rust.

Many have been meticulously restored, often by specialist Roberto Negri who knows the cars inside out having worked for Iso in period.

Once returned to good condition, a Grifo still makes for a reliable grand tourer with genuine continent crossing ability thanks to its beefy American mechanicals – and head turning looks courtesy of its blue-chip Italian lineage.

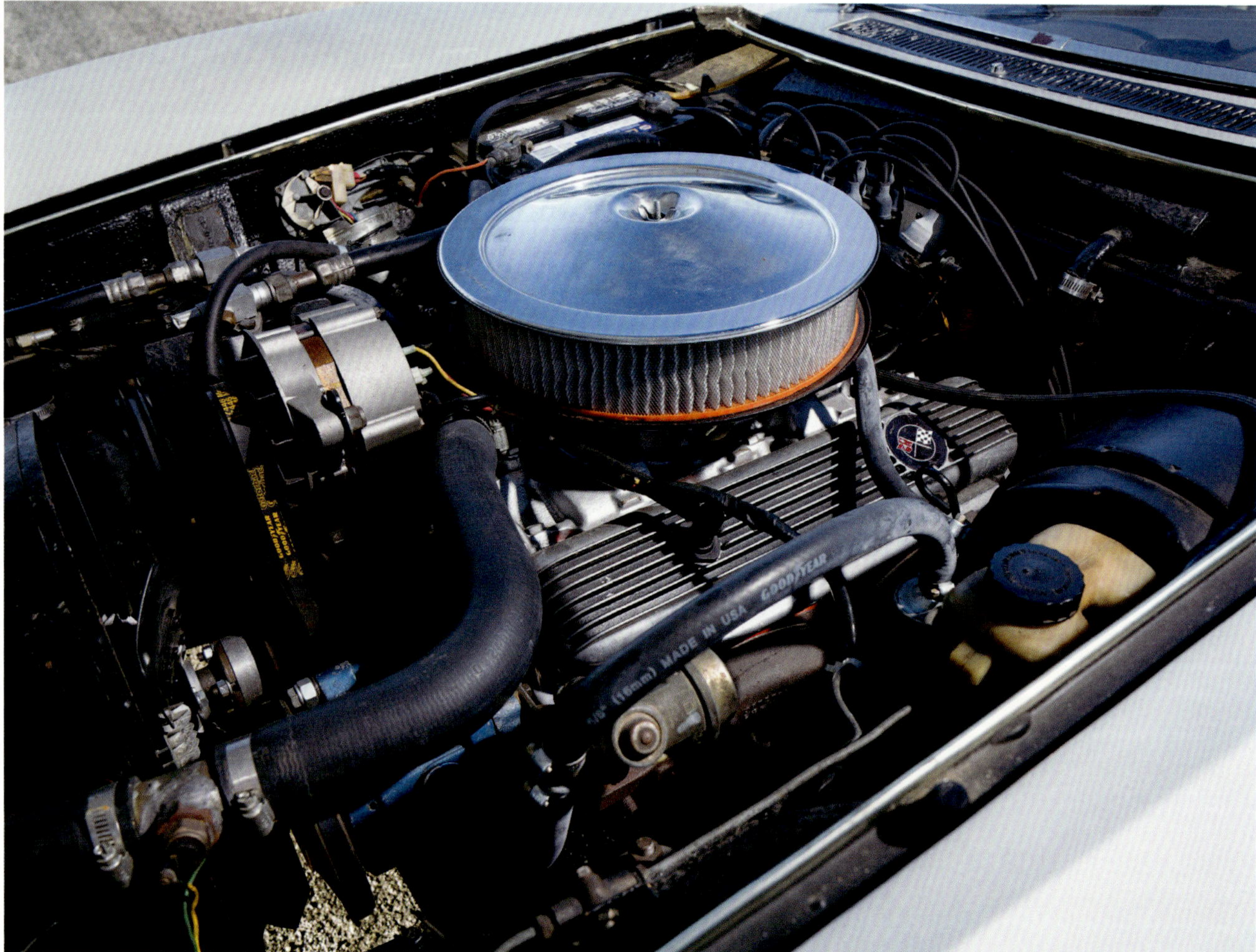
MADE IN USA GOODYEAR

Porsche 911 2.7 RS

Production dates: 1972 - 1973
Number built: 1,580
Designer: Ferdinand A. Porsche
Engine: 2.7 litre, six cylinder
Fuel consumption: 20 - 30 mpg
Top speed: 150 mph

There is a (probably apocryphal) story about the celebrated German academic and industrial designer Dr Dieter Rams being asked by a journalist why he chose to drive a Porsche 911. On hearing the question, he looked at his interlocutor with a somewhat perplexed expression before replying: "Because it is clearly the most efficient means of travelling quickly by road from A to B that has yet been invented."

Regardless of whether or not the tale is true, the 911 set a new benchmark for road-going sports cars when it arrived on the scene in 1963 thanks to its unrivalled combination of performance, reliablity, handling, build quality and sheer 'drivability' that made it as suitable for nipping to the shops as it was for competing in an international rally.

It was all the more remarkable, then, that Porsche was able to produce a special 'extreme' version of the 911 that delivered more power and speed while retaining the standard car's tractability.

Launched in 1972 at the Paris auto show, the Carrera 2.7 RS (for 'rennsport, or 'racing sport) was intended purely for competition use, but Porsche was obliged to build 500 road-going examples in order to homologate the model for the Group 4 GT category.

The expectation was that few people would be interested in buying one for road use due to the stripped-out, minimalist specification, and there were fears among the management that shifting 500 might be a struggle. But 51 cars were sold during the show alone, with the remaining 449 being snapped-up within a week.

Indeed, such was the demand for the RS that Porsche only stopped production after 1,580 had rolled off the line, much of the model's appeal lying in the fact that it combined 150mph performance with the standard car's reliability and surprising economy, meaning it was as practical as ever – but even more fun.

The markedly improved performance was achieved by increasing engine capacity from the 2.4 litres of the standard car to 2.7 litres and the fitment of Bosch mechanical fuel injection, resulting in an output of 210 horsepower. This was combined with a significant weight reduction over the normal 'S' model on which the car was based, thanks to the use of thinner steel for the bodywork, lighter 'Glaverbell' glass and polyester bumpers.

Other modifications included the fitment of wider rear wheels and a distinctive 'ducktail' spoiler to the engine cover – a stylish aerodynamic tweak that is said to have added 2mph to the car's top speed.

The RS was offered in two specifications, 'lightweight' and 'touring', the latter benefiting from the addition – at extra cost – of features such as sunroofs, sun visors, head linings and sound proofing. In either form, a 2.7 RS is today considered one of the most desirable and usable of all classic cars, and most serious collectors want one in their motorhouse.

However, there are more than 1, 580 serious collectors in the world, leading to a 'supply and demand' situation that has pushed the values of the best examples well beyond the £500,000 mark.

"It is clearly the most efficient means of travelling quickly by road from A to B that has yet been invented."

Carrera

RS·911

Jensen Interceptor

Production dates: 1966 - 1976
Number built: 6,408
Designer: Carrozeria Touring
Engine: 5.9 litre, 6.3 litre, 7.2 litre V8
Fuel consumption: 10 - 15 mpg
Top speed: 135 mph

"He kept her in a Jensen Interceptor, delivered her with roses to my door..." So sang the Welsh rock 'n' roller Dave Edmunds in 'Goodbye Mr Good Guy' on his 1979 album *Repeat When Necessary*.

The relevance of the car to the rest of the lyrics is not entirely obvious – but it's probably true to say that, while the Jaguar E-Type was often regarded as a carriage for the sporting gentleman, a muscle-bound Interceptor held more appeal to the fast-driving cad rather than any 'Mr Good Guy' type.

Although launched in 1966, the Interceptor seems very much a car of the '70s, despite it being a decade in which soaring fuel prices considerably blunted the appeal of gas-guzzling grand tourers.

And Jensens sure could guzzle because, despite hailing from the Midlands town of West Bromwich, they packed American-built Chrysler V8 engines that ranged in capacity from 6.3 litres to 7.2 litres, imbuing the car with a top speed of an easy 135mph and truly blistering acceleration.

When the throttle was mashed, the engines' massive torque also had the ability to make Interceptor passengers feel as though their stomachs had been displaced to the nether regions of the car's remarkably innovative (and wholly practical) body that was designed by Carrozeria Touring of Italy and featured an impressively large cargo area accessed from a hatchback fitted with a distinctive expanse of wraparound glass.

In fact, 'innovation' was a byword for the Interceptor, which sported a beautifully crafted instrument panel reminiscent of the flight deck of a light aircraft, ahead-of-their time anti-lock brakes and, on the F/F model, a four-wheel-drive system that preceded the production version of Audi's celebrated 'Quattro' set-up by more than a decade.

That greedy engine – which supped petrol at the rate of 10mpg when asked to really perform – meant Interceptor buyers needed to be wealthy, not only to buy them but also to run them.

As a result, the car attracted many high-profile owners, ranging from Frank Sinatra, Tony Curtis and Clark Gable to *Carpetbaggers* author Harold Robbins, *Sweeney* actor John Thaw, boxer Henry Cooper and Led Zeppelin drummer John Bonham (who was a particular fan, getting through no fewer than seven Interceptors despite dying at the young age of 32).

Although the hatchback body style is considered 'classic' Interceptor, the car was also made as a convertible and, in very limited numbers, as a so-called 'coupé' with a rear screen from a Jaguar XJ6 and a lift-out roof panel.

Those who found the muscle provided by the standard engine a little lacking, meanwhile, were offered a souped-up version for 1971 called the SP – which stood for 'Six Pack', a term that alluded to the use of three, two-barrel carburettors atop the 7.2-litre engine.

It was a simple tweak that upped output from 305 to 330 horsepower to create the most powerful Jensen ever and, while most Interceptors were supplied with tough, TorqueFlight three-speed automatic

transmissions, a few buyers went for the manual gearbox option that made the car even more of a hot rod.

But despite the Interceptor's many appealing qualities, Jensen went bust in 1975 and the once audacious grand tourer looked set to be consigned to the mists of time as used values plummeted and neglected examples were left to succumb to the rust that was always the car's Achilles heel.

In recent years, however, the true wonder of this elegant, ahead-of-its time mile-muncher has come to be appreciated, and now everyone seems to want an Interceptor in their garage.

Even good guys...

"He kept her in a Jensen Interceptor, delivered her with roses to my door..."

10 MOK

Datsun 240Z

Production dates: 1969 - 1973
Number built: 164,616
Designer: Albrecht Goertz and Yoshiko Matsuo
Engine: 2.4 litre, six cylinder
Fuel consumption: 20 - 25 mpg
Top speed: 125 mph

Just as we Brits didn't believe the Japanese could teach us much about building motorcycles before the likes of Honda, Yamaha and Suzuki began to dominate the racing scene during the 1960s, so we didn't think the engineers from the Land of the Rising Sun would ever be able to build a decent sports car. Until, that is, the swooping lines of the Datsun 240Z hove into view at the end of 1969.

Until then, Japanese manufacturers were best known for making reliable but bland commuter cars, with only Toyota having a go at the conventional, full-sized sports sector with its limited production 2000GT made famous in the James Bond film *You Only Live Twice*, while Honda had its S600 'micro' car and Mazda its complex and expensive rotary-engined Cosmo.

The 240Z, however, posed a direct challenge to established sportsters such as the MGB GT and the Triumph GT6 by offering a punchy, six-cylinder engine, a beautifully designed coupé body with a practical hatchback, finely balanced handling – and a level of build quality and reliability that English and European manufacturers just couldn't match.

In Japan the car was known as the 'Fairlady Z' and could only be bought from special dealerships called Nissan Bluebird Stores – but mainland Europe and north America were the main targets for the new model where it was called the '240Z', the name denoting the 2.4 litres of its 150 horsepower motor that gave the car a top speed of a genuine 125mph.

Race-style bucket seats, a comprehensive instrument panel with dash-top binnacles and a silky, short-throw gearbox gave the Z a truly sporting feel – and quickly left the opposition appearing hopelessly outdated, especially in the refinement of its mechanicals and the quality of its electrical systems that made those of the British seem thoroughly antiquated.

The car's aforementioned balance and the fact that many of its underpinnings were from the robust 510 saloon (which had proved itself as a race car) also made it a favourite among competitive drivers. Hollywood star Paul Newman was one of those who achieved notable successes in 240Zs while driving for the Bob Sharp Racing team.

If you didn't feel a standard 240Z was quite quick enough, however, a British specialist called Spike Anderson offered highly tuned 'Super Samuri' [*sic*] versions that proved to be a force to be reckoned with on the country's race circuits and can now be worth double the amount of a standard Z. The 'Samuri' name was not a result of Anderson being unable to spell correctly, by the way – it was to do with the fact that someone else had already trademarked 'Samurai'.

In 1974, the Z had its engine capacity upped to 2.6 litres and was then made available as a 'two-plus-two' version with occasional rear seats – but the arrival of the even larger-engined 280Z in 1975 signalled the beginning of the end of the original prior to the arrival, in 1978, of the larger, less svelte 280 ZX.

When it emerged in the late 1990s that people still held a soft spot for the 240, however, Datsun (by then universally known as Nissan) attempted to create a 'heritage' version by buying back tired examples and restoring them to as-new condition, then offering them to dealers for around $25,000.

The plan did not prove popular and fewer than 50 were sold. If this idea was revisited today, however, the outcome might be rather different...

Perhaps the greatest testament to the sheer toughness of the Z was its victory in the gruelling 21st East African Safari Rally of 1973 in the hands of Kenyan ace Shekhar Mehtar.

DATSUN

BMW 3.0 CSL

Production dates: 1971 - 1974
Number built: 1,208
Designer: Karmann
Engine: 3.0 litre, six cylinder
Fuel consumption: 18 - 25 mpg
Top speed: 135 mph

With acres of glass making for a light-filled interior, a long wheelbase to provide both legroom and a comfortable ride and a silky-smooth, three-litre, fuel injected engine for effortless cruising, BMW's new, Karmann-styled 3.0 CS coupé of 1968 was sporty, good-looking and decidedly capable.

But the marque's competition department believed the new flagship had potential beyond simply being an autobahn stormer and decided to create an even more impressive version to homologate in order that it could contest the prestigious European Touring Car Championship.

The result added something to the model name – the letter 'L' – while also taking something away: weight. The 'L' stood for 'leichtmetall' and referred to the substitution of the standard car's steel doors, bonnet and boot lid for thin-gauge aluminium, changing the glass side windows for Perspex, fitting lightweight bucket seats and, for home market models, ditching creature comforts such as carpets and electric windows.

The work trimmed a useful 300lbs from the standard weight, while engines produced 206 horsepower in road-going cars and in excess of 300 horsepower when tuned for racing.

Much of the work was carried out in collaboration with a German engineer called Burkard Bovensiepen who, a few years before the production 3.0 CS was launched, had shown a knack for making standard BMWs go faster by developing a tuning kit for the 1500 model in a shed at the back of his family's typewriter factory in Buchloe.

Within three years Bovensiepen had ditched the typewriters in order to focus on developing performance parts for BMWs under the Alpina brand name, an enterprise that proved so successful that drivers such as Derek Bell, James Hunt, Niki Lauda and Jackie Ickx began racing Alpina-tuned BMWs. Between them they gained the small firm a raft of touring car victories during the late 1960s and early '70s.

And it was Alpina's involvement with the 3.0 CSL project that, in 1973, resulted in the creation of the so-called 'Batmobile' aerodynamic package developed in conjunction with Stuttgart University. This meant the addition of a front spoiler, fin-like tops on the front wings, another spoiler mounted above the rear window and, most ostentatious of all, a giant rear wing mounted on the boot.

It might have looked like a case of 'go faster stripes' gone mad – but the kit proved so effective that the new Batmobiles trounced everything in their wake to capture no fewer than six wins in the European Touring Car Championship and secure a class win at the 1973 Le Mans 24 Hours.

In order to achieve homologation for racing, at least 500 road cars had to be made available with the same equipment used on the racers. In Germany, however, it was illegal to use such aerodynamic devices on the highway, so the Batmobiles were delivered with their spoilers stowed away, neatly wrapped in the boot for later fitting at the owner's discretion.

CSL models that have remained in standard condition and retain the aerodynamic 'kit' have subsequently gone on to prove that less (weight) can mean more (money) – because the best now change hands for up to £250,000.

More or less priceless, however, are the two CSL racers painted by Alexander Calder and Frank Stella that became the first of BMW's celebrated series of 'Art Cars'.

Lancia Stratos

Production dates: 1973-1978
Number built: 492
Designer: Marcello Gandini for Bertone
Engine: 2.4 litre, six cylinder
Fuel consumption: 18 mpg
Top speed: 140 mph

The design might now be more than 40 years old, but few would disagree that Lancia's wild and crazy Stratos somehow looks futuristic even by today's standards. It's hardly surprising that the car has stood the test of time, however – it was designed by Marcello Gandini of Bertone who had already penned such smash hits as Lamborghini's Miura and Countach models.

Visitors must have been agog at the sight of the radical new car when the prototype was unveiled at the 1971 Turin Motor Show, not least because it would have seemed light years ahead of the old fashioned Fulvia Coupé that it was set to replace as Lancia's rally weapon.

When the production model emerged two years later, the look had barely changed. Still there was the prototype's jet fighter style, wraparound windscreen and it remained virtually impossible to see anything 'out the back' – but the finished product didn't make do with the originally proposed Lancia engine, being fitted instead with the same Ferrari V6 found in the Prancing Horse marque's outgoing Dino model.

The combination of the 190 horsepower motor, a sub-1,000kg kerb weight and miniscule dimensions resulted in a car for which the term 'pocket rocket' might have been invented – and it admirably served the purpose for which it was built, trouncing the opposition and thrilling the crowds with a remarkable 19 wins in World Rally Championship events between 1974 and 1981 and achieving overall championship victories in 1974, '75 and '76.

But, while the 'standard' HF Stradale road cars built to bring-up the homologation numbers produced around 190 horsepower and managed a top speed of 140mph, the highly tuned factory versions put out nearer 300 horsepower, with a pair of turbocharged models intended for Group 5 circuit racing creating a remarkable, if virtually uncontrollable, 560 horsepower.

As a practical proposition for travelling from A to B at normal speeds among normal traffic, however, the Stratos was entirely unsuitable. Its tiny cockpit was claustrophobic and its plastic windows, partly glass-fibre bodywork and flip-up engine cover did little to deaden the din of the screaming engine positioned inches behind the close-coupled seats. The driving position, meanwhile, was close to prone and, like many Italian sports cars, the control pedals were crammed together and offset at peculiar angles.

The result was that normal 'Stradale' versions proved difficult to shift, with brand new examples still being available to buy – usually at considerable discounts – two years after production ceased in 1978.

However, with its superb rallying history, unique looks, impressive performance and low production numbers, the Stratos has since become one of the most sought-after collector's cars of its era that buyers now willingly pay upwards of £250,000 to own.

One particular enthusiast, car designer Christian Hrabalek, likes them so much that he has acquired 11, while Richard Mille, the founder of the eponymous luxury watch brand, has two in matching Alitalia rally livery – one of which won the San Remo rally in both 1975 and 1976 in the hands of the late Swedish star Bjorn Waldegard.

Mr Mille now uses it for nipping to the shops near his chateau outside Rennes ... and almost always drives the long way home.

HF

Y70340 ROMA
Y70340

ACQUA °C
TEMP OLIO °C
BENZINA
LANCIA
FISPA
FILTRO ARIA A SECCO
SOSTITUIRE LA CARTUCCIA OGNI 10.000 Km.
DRY AIR CLEANER
FIAMM

Citroën SM

Production dates: 1970 - 1974
Number built: 12,854
Designer: Robert Opron with Henri de Ségur Lauve
Engine: 2.7 litre (later cars 3.0 litre) V6
Fuel consumption: 18 mpg
Top speed: 140 mph

What could possibly go wrong in a marriage that combined quirky French design with temperamental Italian engineering? It's a question that nobody seems to have asked before the decision was made to develop the Maserati-powered Citroën SM shortly after the French car giant acquired the then-ailing Trident marque in 1968.

Having already spent most of the decade pondering the possibilities of creating a sporting version of the technically brilliant DS, Citroën suddenly found the solution for how to do it sitting right at its fingertips in the combination of a Maserati motor and new, DS-inspired coupé bodywork penned by in-house designer Robert Opron and consultant Henri de Ségur Lauve.

With its six headlamps (two of which swivelled in synchronicity with the front wheels) a swooping, aerodynamic silhouette, self-levelling, hydro-pneumatic suspension and 'variable' power steering that became lighter as the car went slower, the SM's space-age spec. caused gasps of amazement when it was unveiled at the Geneva motor show in 1970 as the first true sports car in decades to have been produced by a major French maker.

As well as giving the Citroën line-up a sporting offering, the SM was also intended to bring some glamour to the brand while enhancing its appeal in the important North American market.

Most large gran turismos of the time, however, boasted suitably large-capacity engines – but French tax laws favoured smaller units, leading the SM's designers to take a 4.2 litre Maserati V8 and lop-off two cylinders to create a quad-cam, 90-degree V6 of 2,670cc, which slipped in nicely below the 16CV fiscal rating to avoid the sort of punitive taxation that would have made the car all but impossible to sell.

Although the SM was large and heavy, the Maserati engine's 170 horsepower proved enough to give the car a level of speed and acceleration that more or less matched its rocket ship looks, while the superbly comfortable interior and brilliant suspension made covering big distances at high speed enjoyably effortless.

But, while it might have seemed like a recipe for unqualified success, the SM proved difficult to shift. Some say Citroën dealers simply weren't up to working with the type of customers who were used to buying cars from Porsche or Mercedes, while others say the firm's service network made an unnecessary meal of the perceived complexity of having to deal with an engine designed by Maserati.

Additionally, US sales were killed by laws introduced for the 1974 model year that required bumpers to be of a specific height and able to sustain a 5mph impact without damage to the car's lights, safety equipment or engine. The SM's couldn't, so Citroën withdrew the remaining 130 or so examples from sale and sent them to Japan, leading to the closure of the SM factory in Paris shortly afterwards.

But despite its too-short life, the exotic SM can claim to have gone a long way to bringing Citroën the up-market status to which it aspired, attracting famous owners such as Emperor Haile Selassie of Ethiopia, Rolling Stone Bill Wyman, author Graham Greene and musician Carlos Santana.

Among more infamous fans, meanwhile, was the Ugandan dictator Idi Amin – who acquired seven for 'state use'.

Today, SM's are highly collectable with the most valuable being the seven convertible 'Mylord' versions created by coachbuilder Henri Chapron., the last of which realised Euros 548,000 when it crossed the auction block at Artcurial in Paris in 2014. A standard SM can be had for around £20,000

The superbly comfortable interior and brilliant suspension made covering big distances at high speed enjoyably effortless.

M.BOTTER
INJECTION ELECTRONIQUE
CITROEN

1980s

DeLorean DMC 12

Production dates: 1981 - 1983
Number built: 9,200
Designer: Bill Collibs, Colin Chapman, Giugiaro
Engine: 2.9 litre V6
Fuel consumption: 21 mpg
Top speed: 115 mph

Fans of the hit movie *Back to the Future* will not need reminding of the importance of the DeLorean motor car which, had it not been for its starring role as Doc Brown's four-wheeled time machine, might merely have entered the history books as one of the great automotive failures of the late 20th century.

For those unfamiliar with the DeLorean DMC 12, it was the brainchild of former Chevrolet general manager John Z. Delorean whose aim was to build 'the ethical sports car for the bachelor who's made it'.

Having touted the idea around the world, Delorean finally persuaded the British Government that the undeniably different car was set to be a smash hit that would bring steady employment and untold returns to the area in which it was built.

As a result, a Northern Irish production line was set-up in Dunmurry – a suburb of the terrorism-troubled city of Belfast – using $175 million of (mostly) other people's money. High unemployment in the area made for no shortage of applicants for the well-paid jobs available at the factory, but few of those who were taken on had any experience at all of motor manufacture.

The car they were tasked to build had originally been drafted by former Pontiac engineer Bill Collins before having its underpinnings and suspension heavily re-worked by Lotus founder Colin Chapman. It featured Giugiaro-designed gull-wing body-work in brushed stainless steel and a rather unglamorous rear-mounted, 2.9-litre engine supplied by the Peugeot/Renault group.

The interior, meanwhile, had high-tech pretensions with its tilting, telescopic steering column, complex ventilation system and multi-position climate control. However, those gullwing doors proved problematic and, despite being 'double-sealed', they were prone to leaks and needed to be approached with caution since the feeble, gas-filled struts intended to hold them up had a habit of collapsing unexpectedly.

Despite the car's failings, the DeLorean factory produced 9,200 DMC 12s before going bust in late 1982 after the marque's founder was caught in an FBI sting agreeing to bankroll a somewhat unethical $1.8 million cocaine smuggling operation – although he was subsequently found not guilty on the basis of illegal entrapment.

Under different circumstances and with better guidance, the car had the potential to be a far greater success. Offering a top sped of 115mph, it was small and good-looking while being surprisingly practical – not only could it accommodate two six-footers, it was designed to have sufficient space behind the front seats to carry a full set of golf clubs.

For more than two decades after production ended, the DMC 12 remained an oddity that inspired affection because of its starring role in *Back to the Future* but was far from being sought after by collectors. But that's changed of late and the best now command up to £50,000.

And, if you want to experience a new DeLorean, Liverpudlian Stephen Wynne might be able to sell you one... Having acquired the entire inventory of DeLorean bodies and parts after the original firm went bust, Wynne hopes to start making new DMC 12s in Texas following a change in US law which allows manufacturers to produce 325 examples annually of a car originally made more than 25 years ago provided it complies with current emissions standards.

DMC

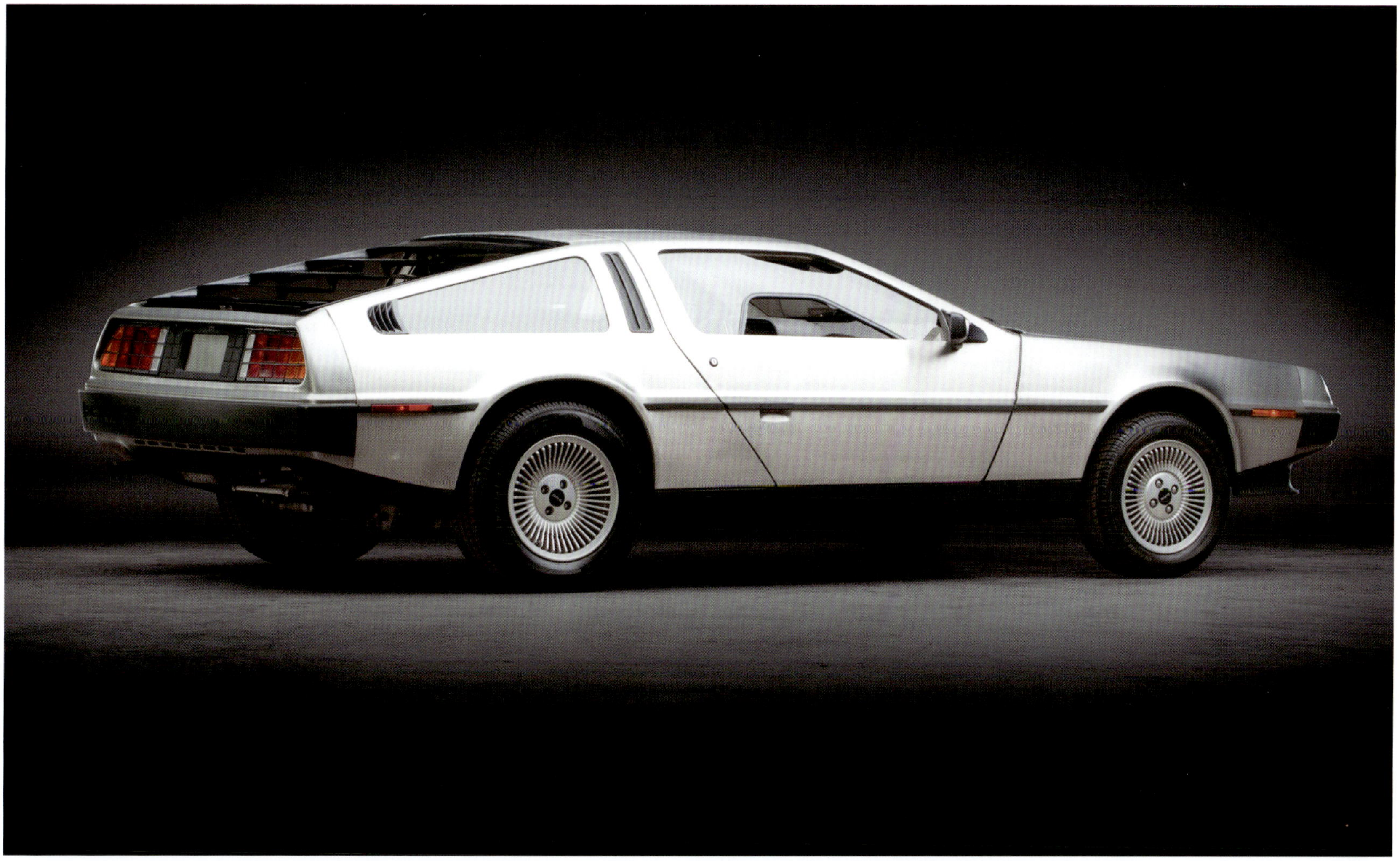

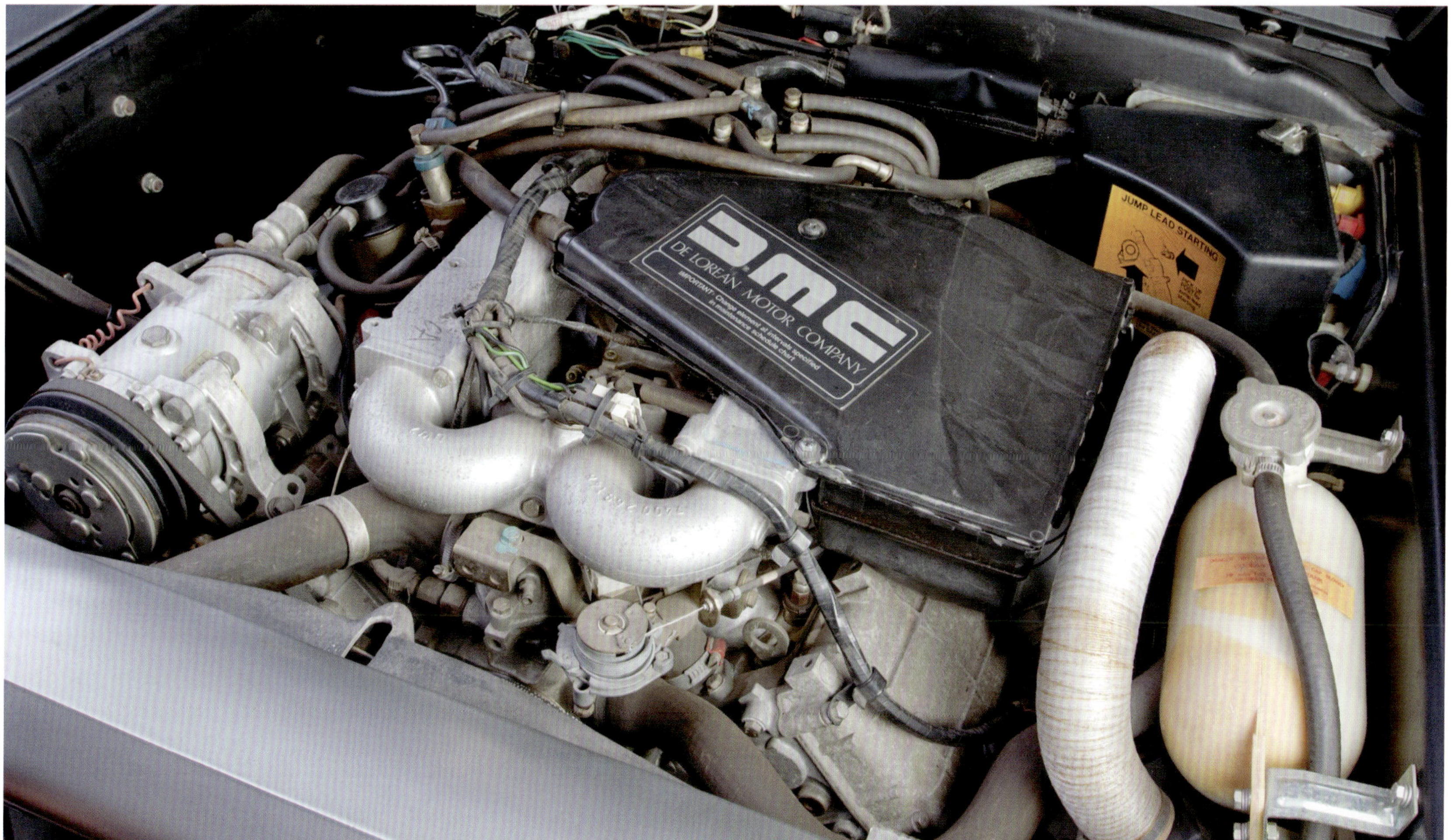
DE LOREAN MOTOR COMPANY
JUMP LEAD STARTING

Rolls-Royce Camargue

Number built: 531
Designer: Pininfarina
Engine: 6.75 litre V8
Fuel consumption: 15 mpg
Top speed: 115 mph

They do say some things improve with age, and the Rolls-Royce Camargue might just be one of them. Shamelessly launched in 1975 not long after the Opec oil crisis had seen the cost of a barrel of crude quadruple in the space of a year and caused a stock market crash, the large and ostentatious two-door was aimed fairly and squarely at people who were wealthy enough not to care how much it cost to run. Or how much it cost to buy.

Initially priced at £29,250, the Camargue could lay claim to being the most expensive production car in the world back then, the sum being the equivalent today of roughly £250,000.

For the first time since the war, Rolls-Royce outsourced the design, handing the commission to the celebrated Italian stylist Pininfarina – which, in the eyes of many critics, produced one of the least attractive automobiles of all time.

The lumbering coupé bodywork featured the first sloping example of the famous radiator grille at the front, the swage line following through to a clumsy rear end that was completed by lights that would not have looked out of place on a light commercial vehicle. Even the car's wheels seemed a bit wrong, appearing too small to be able to support its bulk.

Regardless of its looks, however, the Camargue had presence to spare – and beneath its vast bonnet lurked Rolls-Royce's venerable 'L' series 6.75-litre, V8 engine that could trace its lineage right back to 1950.

Inside, occupants were cosseted to the usual Rolls-Royce levels of 'drawing room' luxury with what was essentially a hide-covered three-piece-suite that looked out on a dashboard combining Old World walnut veneer with a modernist instrument layout that included a large outside temperature thermometer and the two sets of controls required to operate the first-of-a-kind split-level climate control system.

Supplied with an FM radio as standard, the Camargue also featured dashboard blanking plates that could be removed to enable the installation of a cassette player and an eight-track cartridge system to provide the full spectrum of in-car entertainment – although the usual Rolls-Royce bespoke service meant Sir or Madame could specify virtually any other extras they required (for an additional consideration, of course).

To those who knew, however, the Camargue's imposing coupé bodywork was little more than a different skin atop the underpinnings used for the four-door Silver Shadow and the two-door Corniche (which the Camargue was intended to replace). It did, however, cost twice as much as the Corniche which, most would agree, looked ten times nicer.

However, that was then and this is now... Despite the Carmague making it into books such as *The 100 Worst Cars Ever* and magazine lists of 'uncool' wheels, people are recognising it as being a noble, majestic and rather rare oddity that makes as much of a statement today as it did over 40 years ago.

You can now buy a Camargue for the same price as a moderate family hatchback...

H.R.OWEN

C822 KAX

Ferrari 288 GTO

Production dates: 1984 - 1985
Number built: 272
Designer: Leonardo Fioravanti for Pininfarina
Engine: 2.8 litre V8
Fuel consumption: 15 mpg
Top speed: 185 mph

Just like the legendary 250 GTO of the 1960s, Ferrari's 288 GTO was built as a 'homologation special', this time to enable the Prancing Horse marque to take part in the FIA's Group B circuit race series proposed in 1982 that required competing cars to have been made in a minimum of 200 examples and be capable of being legally driven on the road, complete with full instruments, lights, windscreen wipers, rear view mirrors and a practical degree of ground clearance.

Although Group B rallying took off and provided some of the most spectacular and entertaining motorsport of all time, the circuit race series failed to make it out of the starting blocks – meaning every one of the fire-breathing 288 GTOs built ended up being registered for the road.

Despite being loosely based on the existing 308 and 328 designs, the car was almost entirely different thanks to the use of lightweight, composite body panels with oblique rear wing vents, pumped-up wheel arches, quadruple driving lights and a version of the subtle rear spoiler first seen on the 250 GTO.

Even the car's wheels were unique, being specially designed, five-spoke magnesium alloy Speedline split rims that were wider at the front than at the back and held in place, race style, by a single, quick-release nut.

Beneath the engine cover could be found a jewel-like V8 motor displacing just 2.9 litres but packing a knockout punch thanks to the addition of fuel injection and not one, but two IHI turbochargers – features that required the lateral mounting set-up used in the 308/328 to be altered to longitudinal mounting with the gearbox and differential behind.

The result was was nothing short of thrilling to drive, its engine producing 400 turbo-boosted horsepower at a screaming 7,000rpm and making the 288 GTO the first road-going production car to top 300kmh.

With the promise of such performance and the looks to match, demand for the 288 GTO exceeded the originally intended number of 200, meaning a further 72 were built, with every car being sold before it was made. This was despite the fact that the model was only available with 'Rosso' paintwork, the limited options being a choice of all-leather seats or orange squabs, electric windows, air conditioning and a radio.

What was perhaps most remarkable about the 288 GTO, however, was that it combined a race-bred pedigree and striking looks with the tractability to be driven on public roads – a characteristic that made it the forerunner of today's breed of limited edition 'supercars' which high-end marques make available in limited numbers for their most valued customers.

When new, a 288 GTO cost around £60,000. The model became collectable almost instantly and, during the late 1980s values soared to almost £1m before falling dramatically when the classic car bubble burst. Since the turn of the century, however, prices have climbed steadily, to the point that an entry level car now costs around £1 million, with the very best of the best commanding close to twice as much.

pininfarina

GTO

Jaguar XJS

Production dates: 1975 - 1996
Number built: 115,413
Designer: Malcolm Sayer and Doug Thorpe
Engine: 5.3 litre V12, 6 litre V12; 3.6 litre six cylinder, 4 litre six cylinder
Fuel consumption: 15 - 30 mpg
Top speed: 150 mph

Any car intended to replace the legendary Jaguar E-Type had giant-sized shoes to fill – and many people thought the XJ-S might not be up to the job when it was launched in 1975, not least a straight-talking journalist from *Car* magazine who wrote: 'The Jaguar XJ-S's most glaring fault – its ugliness.'

Well, they do say that beauty is subjective, but one can't help wondering whether or not such a harsh summation was more to do with a refusal to accept that anything could serve as a worthy successor to the beloved E-Type, especially not a car that cost twice the price.

Most people who complained about the XJ-S aesthetic, however, started with the unusual 'buttresses' that tapered from the top of the roof pillar to the rear lights. Different, yes, but hardly 'ugly'. In fact, examination of the car from virtually any angle these days reveals it to be rather beautiful, its unusual oval headlamps connected by a slim radiator grille lending a distinctly (and probably intentional) feline air.

Then there was the gracefully curved rear window inset between those controversial buttresses, the special alloy wheels, the two small-bore tail pipes and the black bumpers, window frames, chin spoiler and rear air vents that added a racy touch to a car that was always intended to be more of a continent-crossing grand tourer than outright sportster.

Those GT credentials were enhanced by a sensibly sized boot, small but adequate rear seats, an almost eerily quiet cabin and – the car's real forte – a silky-smooth, 5.3 litre V12 engine that gave the XJ-S a top speed in excess of 150mph and enabled it to cruise at three-figure speeds without breaking sweat.

Overall it oozed quality, from the heavy chrome of the door mirrors to the depth of the paint and from the smell of the hide to the reassuring weight of the gear selector.

As with many similar cars of its era, however, the XJ-S landed in the wake of a fuel crisis that dented the popularity of such large-engined GTs, few of which came more thirsty.

Its 'gentleman's express' image was given a boost when it was selected to transport Simon Templar in the television series *Return of the Saint* (the car was white, of course), and when Mike Gambit was given a red one to drive in *The New Avengers*.

In 1981, the fuel consumption was half-heartedly addressed with the introduction of the so-called 'High Efficiency' engine – capable of a claimed 20mpg – but the arrival of a 3.6-litre, six-cylinder version two years later really did make the XJ-S relatively frugal. An SC 'cabriolet' followed, as well as a full convertible and a souped-up XJR-S model developed in conjunction with Tom Walkinshaw Racing which had enjoyed considerable success with Jaguars on the track.

A full makeover happened in 1991 that included a name change from XJ-S to XJS, before a series of 'Celebration' editions was launched in 1995 to signal the end of production.

Some of the best XJ-S/XJS cars were not, however, those made by Jaguar but were aftermarket conversions. One, the Lynx Eventer, turned the coupé into a rapid shooting brake, while Lister created a highly tuned, 7-litre version with bulging wheel arches and top speed of 170mph.

But by the turn of the 21st century, the XJS/-S had come to be deemed a gas-guzzling irrelevance and a decent one could be picked-up for around £1,500.

It's a different story now, however – the best of the best regularly realise £40,000-plus, with examples of the rare Eventer fetching even more.

AD 208 VK

JAGUAR V12
SATTIN
AUTOFFICINA
BRAKE SYSTEM WARNING

Audi Quattro

Production dates: 1980 - 1991
Number built: 11,452
Designer: Ferdinand Piëch and Martin Smith
Engine: 2.1 litre, 2.2 litre, five cylinder turbocharged
Fuel consumption: 15 - 30 mpg
Top speed: 130 - 150 mph

Few 'modern classics' have names that resonate as strongly as Audi's Quattro. Originally conceived as a high-performance road car, it shared the bodyshell and many other parts with the standard GT hatchback coupé – but the addition of a turbocharger to the GT's 2.1 litre, five-cylinder engine and an upgrade to permanent four-wheel-drive made for a different beast altogether.

British designer Martin Smith was tasked with making the car stand out from the 'cooking' GT, a job he addressed by modifying the standard front and rear wings with distinctive, flat-topped bulges that drew the eye towards the wheels, thereby emphasising its 'Quattro' specification.

With 200 horsepower on tap and a top speed of more than 135mph – plus four-wheel-drive roadholding that no other production car could match – the Quattro proved to be a veritable rocket ship, especially in the hands of a skilled driver on a twisty road. And that unusual, five-cylinder engine configuration made for a unique and thrilling sound, too.

It was natural, therefore, that the Quattro should quickly find its way onto the racetrack, initially with its engine tuned to around 300 horsepower. It soon showed its mettle, with female driver Michèle Mouton becoming the first woman to win a world championship rally when she took a Quattro to victory in the 1981 San Remo event.

That, however, was just the start of a glittering rally history that saw specially developed versions of the Quattro contest the thrilling Group B category, with celebrated drivers such as Stig Blomqvist, Hannu Mikkola and Walter Röhrl piloting the famous 'S1' short wheelbase, kevlar-bodied, 450 horsepower cars to numerous victories in the world's most high-profile events.

These latter cars – which were decidedly more workmanlike than good-looking – were made available to the general public as road-going 'homologation' specials,' complete with huge rally arches to accommodate their extra-wide wheels and notably steeper windscreens borrowed from the Audi 80 saloon to improve visibility.

One of these also won the gruelling Pikes Peak International Hill Climb in 1985, again with Michèle Mouton at the wheel. Back then, the 12.4 mile course with its 156 turns consisted almost entirely of loose dirt – but Mouton's tenacious Quattro still made it to the top in a record time of 11 minutes, 25 seconds. In total, Quattros won the event no fewer than five times between 1982 and 1987, only missing out in 1984 to a purpose-built, single-seater Wells Coyote.

Today, there are few performance car enthusiasts who would not wish to have an Audi Quattro in their collection – but examples of the 224 short wheelbase versions are regarded as the ultimate. The most paid for one to date is £350,000, ten times what a 'standard' Quattro might be expected to sell for.

C781 FDB
Audi Sport

quattro

BMW M1

Production dates: 1979 - 1981
Number built: 431
Designer: Giorgetto Giugiaro
Engine: 3.5 litre, six cylinder
Fuel consumption: 20 - 25 mpg
Top speed: 163 mph

It is difficult to imagine passionate Italian designers and precision-obsessed Teutonic engineers making happy bedfellows, a fact that threatened to make itself plain in the late 1970s when BMW and Lamborghini tried to get together to build a road car in sufficient numbers that it could be homologated to take on rival manufacturer Porsche in Group 5 for racing.

Financial troubles at Lamborghini meant the deal fell apart, but a team of former engineers from the factory founded their own firm called Italengineering and saw the project through to completion, with the car's bodywork being designed by Italy's Giorgetto Giugiaro in the form of a series of glassfibre panels which were attached to an Italian-made, steel space frame chassis by a specialist Italian bonding firm.

After this, the cars were painted and partly trimmed before being sent to Germany where they were completed and fitted with specially hand-built versions of BMW's 3.5 litre, fuel-injected, six-cylinder engine directly behind the cockpit to create the marque's first mid-engined, two-seater.

They do say, however, that too many cooks spoil the broth – and that seemed to have been the case with the M1 because, when the cars were sent to BMW's Munich motorsport department for what should have been a few finishing touches, most were discovered to have been put together in a manner that just wasn't deemed good enough.

In fact, so much tweaking and fettling was required that, by the time they were finished, the rules for the Group 5 race series had changed and the M1 was no longer eligible.

But with a 273 horsepower engine, a top speed of more than 160mph and delightful handling, the M1 simply had too much potential to be left purely as a road car – so a racing programme called ProCar was conceived as a one-make support series to Formula One in which star drivers from various disciplines competed against one another. It ran during the 1979 and 1980 seasons, with the first championship being won by Niki Lauda and the second by Nelson Piquet.

The ProCar M1s were modified versions of the road cars that featured 470 horsepower engines giving a top speed of 191mph. They also had upgraded brakes and suspension, built-in jacks and stripped-out interiors – but the 32 examples resembled the 'standard' M1 sufficiently closely to endow it with the image of a road-going racer and the 399 built quickly found homes and became 'instant classics'.

At an original price of £37,500, they were certainly not cheap – in fact, the equally capable, if not so exotic, Porsche 911 Turbo could be had for £10,000 less. But the M1's rarity, performance and pedigree meant it always maintained its value, finally reaching a temporary plateau in the early 2000s when prices levelled at around £50,000.

Today, however, those who aspire to own one of these rare birds will need at least £350,000 to achieve their M1 dream.

M1

Lotus Turbo Esprit

Production dates: 1980 - 2004
Number built: 7,953 (all engine configurations)
Designer: Giorgetto Giugiaro
Engine: 2.2 litre four cylinder and 3.5 litre V8, turbocharged
Fuel consumption: 20 - 30 mpg
Top speed: 150 - 175 mph

Anyone who has seen the James Bond film *The Spy Who Loved Me* will be familiar with the Lotus Esprit – if not one that was exactly conventional, because Roger Moore's Bond raised more than an eyebrow by driving off the end of a pier in an S1 model that magically transformed into a submarine, having been adapted for the film by Florida-based Perry Oceanographic at a cost of $100,000.

That was in 1977, one year after the Esprit S1 went into production following a seven-year gestation period that began when the Lotus board granted approval for the development of two versions, one with a four-cylinder engine, the other with a V8.

A chance meeting between Lotus founder Colin Chapman and styling genius Giorgetto Giugiaro decided who would pen the car's futuristic, wedge-shaped body which was made from glass fibre and supported on the mark's trademark 'backbone' chassis. This was modified with front and rear subframes that carried the all-independent suspension and the longitudinal, rear-mounted, 2-litre Lotus engine and Citroën gearbox.

The rear lights were borrowed from a Fiat X-19, the wheels were of-the-era Wolfrace slots and the two seats were described by Lotus as being 'hammock-like', giving driver and passenger a semi-recumbent position that emphasised the car's extreme sportiness.

With fabulous looks, sublime handling, a comfortable ride and that legendary Lotus name, the Esprit should have been the ultimate supercar – but with only 160 horsepower on tap in its original form, there was one thing it lacked: serious performance.

That problem was addressed by the factory in 1980 with the arrival of the Turbo Esprit that came with the new. 2.2-litre engine and the useful addition of a turbocharger that instantly boosted power by 30 per cent and sent the top speed soaring from around 130mph to 150mph, slashing almost two seconds of the car's 0-60mph time in the process.

The first models were £21,000 limited editions (the standard car cost around £13,000) and were known as 'Essex Turbos' because they carried the blue, red and chrome livery of Team Lotus sponsor Essex Overseas Petroleum Corporation, with interiors finished in red leather. Just 45 were built, but the car's success both in terms of reception and performance led to the Turbo option being available all the way through the Esprit's remarkable, 28-year production run on cars with both the 2.2-litre engine and later, 3.5-litre V8 models.

James Bond managed to get behind the wheel of not one but two Turbos in 1981's *For Your Eyes Only*, the first being a white version that self destructs, the second a metallic red model that Bond drives, complete with custom-made ski rack, to a mountain resort in Italy.

A less suitable car for use in the snow is difficult to imagine...

turbo
esprit

turbo
esprit

Ford Capri 280 Brooklands

Production dates: 1986 only
Number built: 1,038
Designer: Philip T. Clark
Engine: 2.8 litre, six cylinder
Fuel consumption: 25 - 30 mpg
Top speed: 135 mph

Having observed the stellar trajectory of the best-selling Mustang in America, Ford of Europe set about trying to replicate its success with a 'pony' car of its own, developing a smaller two-door coupé that it had hoped to call – rather unimaginatively – the Colt.

But since that name was already taken by Mitsubishi, an alternative that spoke of the sun-drenched, playboy lifestyle of the Mediterranean was chosen: and so was born the Capri.

Launched in 1968, the Capri soon became a hit, with more than 1.9 million examples being sold in an 18-year production run, ranging from the economy, 1300cc model to regular 1600cc and 2-litre versions, plus some genuine high-performance variants such as the fuel-injected RS2600 of 1971 and the RS3100 that followed a couple of years later.

Ford South Africa even gave its blessing to the aftermarket conversion of around 500 cars by Basil Green Motors in Johannesburg, which added a V8 engine to give a top speed of more than 140mph.

But it was not until 1982 that an off-the-shelf, road-going Capri with really high performance became available with the arrival of the 2.8 Injection model that replaced the old 3-litre and offered a power output of 150 horsepower and a top speed of more than 130mph.

There was a new, five-speed gearbox and an upgraded interior, and the car soon became the basis for various, turbocharged 'specials' from firms such as Tickford and Turbo Technics, the latter making 200 horsepower and 230 horsepower versions that were officially sanctioned by Ford.

All of the above are now highly collectable, but for the Capri purist there is one model that no collection would be complete without – and that is the '280' that was introduced in 1986 as a 'last hurrah' prior to production of the car coming to an end.

Based on the 2.8 Injection, this run-out, ultimate execution was unofficially known as the 'Brooklands' because it was only available in metallic Brooklands Green and featured an all-leather interior with Recaro race-style seats. Other upgrades included a limited-slip differential for improved traction and special, 15-inch diameter alloy wheels.

Most of the 1,038 Capri 280s built were used as they were intended – ie driven hard and fast in all conditions as daily drivers – with the result that many ended up being crashed or run into the ground, while others simply rusted away to the point of having to be scrapped.

Some savvy buyers, however, realised that the final edition of a car as famous as the Capri could only ever rise in value if it was carefully looked after – and now those that survive in excellent, original and preferably unrestored condition fetch sums that even the most optimistic of enthusiasts could never have imagined in 1986.

In 2016, for example, a true 'timewarp' example with just 936 miles on the clock in the hands of its original owner realised £54,000 at auction, while in 2017, a well-cared for 280 with 5,500 miles recorded sold for £47,250.

E28 FNO

280

Ford
F661 RML

1990s

McLaren F1

Production dates: 1993 - 1998
Number built: 106 (includes road and race cars and prototypes)
Designer: Gordon Murray/Peter Stevens
Engine: BMW-designed 6 litre, normally aspirated V12 producing 670 bhp
Fuel consumption: 15 mpg
Top speed: 240 mph (without engine restrictor)

If ever a car defined the term 'modern classic' it is surely the legendary McLaren F1 which, when it went on sale in 1993, carried the then astronomical price tag of £540,000 plus tax. Now, collectors willingly pay £10 million plus for the privilege of owning one of the 105 that were built before production ceased in 1998.

So what's the story behind the car which, almost 20 years later, remains the fastest normally aspirated, street-legal automobile ever made?

According to F1 lore, the model was dreamt up by McLaren Automotive chairman Ron Dennis and legendary racing car design engineer Gordon Murray while they were waiting for a plane following the 1988 Italian Grand Prix. The concept was relatively simple: to create an ultra-high-performance, road-going car that was replete with Formula One technology but that would also be fit for real-world driving.

On March 5 1990, the process of building such a car began. A bespoke twelve-cylinder, non-turbocharged, 6-litre engine producing 627 horsepower had been commissioned from BMW, a six-speed, fast-shifting gearbox was engineered from the ground up, and leading designer Peter Stevens had set-to with his magic pencil to create a body shape the like of which had never before been seen.

Despite being extremely small, the F1 had three seats, with the driver positioned in the middle for optimum balance. It was virtually glued to the ground by Formula One-style downforce enhancement, the mid-engine configuration making for perfect front-to-rear weight distribution and the overall shape being aerodynamically superb.

To ensure maximum driver 'feel', neither brakes nor steering were power-assisted and, as a result of Murray's obsession with lightness, the car was built using exotic materials such as titanium, magnesium and Kevlar. The body panels were made from carbon fibre and, in order to insulate the cockpit from heat, the engine bay was lined with gold foil.

The first F1 was delivered in 1993, production ending five years later after sixty-four road cars, five prototypes, three long-tailed GTS versions made for racing homologation, twenty-eight pure race cars and five Le Mans models had been built – the latter celebrating the F1's victory at the famous 24-hour race in 1995.

On March 31 1998, the F1 established its place in automotive history when a road-going example was taken to a record 240mph, a speed that has only ever been surpassed by cars with turbo-charged engines – yet, ironically, 1998 was also the year when values bottomed out with used cars fetching 'just' £500,000.

Inevitably, however, supply and demand came into play and within a couple of years prices began to creep up. In October 2008, RM Auctions sold the very F1 that for several years had graced McLaren's showroom in London's Park Lane for £2.53m. Then a silver example that had belonged to Oracle CEO Larry Ellison sold for $3.7m and, in 2015, one of the best known of all F1s – the one owned from new by British comedian Rowan Atkinson – was sold privately for £8 million (despite having been heavily crashed on two occasions).

Other celebrated owners of F1s include fashion mogul Ralph Lauren, television star Jay Leno, musician Eric Clapton and Pink Floyd drummer Nick Mason – all of whom, despite their riches, must feel quietly satisfied that the current record price for a McLaren F1 stands at $13.75 million...

Honda NSX

Production dates: 1990 - 2005
Number built: 18,685
Designer: Masahito Nakano and Shigeru Uehara
Engine: 3-litre, six cylinder
Fuel consumption: 20 - 25 mpg
Top speed: 145 mph

Unveiled as a concept in 1989, the original NSX (for NewSportscar – eXperimental) enjoyed a fifteen-year production run from August 1990 to September 2005, during which time more than 18,000 were sold around the world. Originally priced at £52,000, it entered the ring as a serious alternative to cars such as the Ferrari 348 and the Porsche 911, yet many potential buyers struggled to understand how the words 'Honda' and 'supercar' could go hand-in-hand.

But the more open-minded quickly appreciated the fact that this hand-built, mid-engined machine was unique in combining svelte looks, superb handling and a top speed of 180mph (in unrestricted form) with legendary Honda reliability. On top of all that, it featured a look inspired by the cockpit canopy of an F-16 fighter jet, a chassis and suspension set-up developed with the late Formula One star Ayrton Senna, a virtually bullet-proof engine – and was the first mass-produced car to feature an all-aluminium body.

The NSX was easy to drive, too, being as capable of pottering around town as it was of cruising up a motorway or screaming around a race track.

In fact, the NSX completely changed the market because it proved to people who were used to putting up with the quirks and foibles of Lamborghinis and Ferraris that a practical supercar could be a reality. And NSXs remain as usable and as fun to drive today as they were when they were new.

Despite being produced for a relatively long time, there is not a huge variation in models. Early cars had 3-litre engines and a choice of five-speed manual gearboxes or four-speed automatics. In 1995, the NSX-T arrived with a removable roof panel, and, in 1997, the brakes were upgraded and manual cars got 3.2-litre engines and six gears. The most significant change to the appearance of the NSX, meanwhile, came in 2002 when the pop-up headlamps of the original were replaced with fixed units.

Comprehensively equipped as standard in the typical Honda way, the only optional extra available on an export NSX was a CD player – although, from 1993-1996, Japanese buyers were offered the lightweight, track-orientated NSX Type R of which 483 were made with 3-litre engines, followed by 140 fixed headlamp, 3.2-litre models built between 2002 and 2004. Rare, raw and highly sought after, the best of these now change hands for over £200,000.

Evidence of just how good the NSX was – and is – can be seen in the fact that the majority of cars built remain on the road today and are often used by their proud owners as 'daily drivers', with some clocking-up more than 200,000 miles without any apparent loss of performance.

More remarkable still is the fact that, almost 20 years after the end of production, it is still possible to walk into your local Honda dealer and ask for virtually any part for an NSX 'off the shelf'.

M624
PAG

M624 PAG
GB

MG RV8

Production dates: 1993 - 1995
Number built: 1,938
Designer: Syd Enever (design engineer of the MGB)
Engine: 3.9 litre, V8
Fuel consumption: 20 mpg
Top speed: 135 mph

I was walking through Oxford city centre one summer's morning in 1991 when I saw a sports car coast to an ignominious halt on the opposite side of the road. It immediately caught my attention because of its shape, which was somehow very familiar, yet also oddly different.

Keen to see this oddity up close, I crossed the street and began speaking with the car's occupants, two MG engineers who were embarrassed to admit that they had run out of fuel while travelling back to their nearby Abingdon factory at the end of a road test.

Gentle questioning revealed the car to be a prototype of the forthcoming RV8, the two-seat roadster that MG had dreamed-up to compete with the Mazda MX5 which, following its launch in 1989, had caught many rival manufacturers on the back foot with its sensational popularity.

Rather than develop a new car from the ground up, MG Rover's 'Special Products' department opted to allocate £5 million to create an MX5-beater using the basic design of the celebrated 'B' that, by 1991, had been out of production for a decade.

Historic parts supplier British Motor Heritage had already begun to make brand new MGB bodyshells to meet a growing demand from people who wanted to restore cars from the '60s and '70s, and these were chosen as the basis for the RV8 – hence the 'familiar' look – but the styling was updated through the addition of flared front and rear wings that resulted in an altogether more modern and curvaceous appearance.

To ensure hearty performance, power was provided by a version of the Range Rover 3.9-litre, fuel injection engine mated to a five-speed manual gearbox, with the old suspension and braking systems from the 'B' being heavily upgraded to cope. In fact, the car was almost 90 per cent different from the original 'B' despite its obvious family resemblance.

The result was a surprisingly competent package that offered genuine 135mph performance and a well-built feel – although limitations to the car's ride and handling made it more of a 'grand tourer' than an out-and-out sports car in the mould, say, of a TVR.

Had it not been for the fact that it was launched in the midst of the 1992 recession with a £26,000 price tag, the RV8 may well have been a rip-roaring success. In the event, just 1,983 cars were built with the majority (1,581) being sold to Japan where its right-hand-drive configuration fitted in nicely.

Only 311 cars originally found buyers in the UK – but, following a downturn in Japan's economy in 2001, people began to export RV8s back to the UK and Europe where, for many years, they could be bought for around £10,000.

Gradually, however, the performance, quality and rarity of these 'modern classic' MGB-based sports cars has come to be more widely appreciated, and the best now change hands for up to £30,000.

N394
AAW

MG

N394
AAW

Alfa Romeo SZ

Production dates: 1989 - 1991
Number built: 1,036
Designer: Robert Opron
Engine: 3 litre, V6
Fuel consumption: 25 mpg
Top speed: 152 mph

The 1990s was a peculiar era for automotive design, often throwing-up oddities that combined unexpected looks with unusual materials and a degree of technological advancement to create a package that was as likely to leave people puzzled and perplexed as it was to leave them raving with enthusiasm.

One such car was Alfa Romeo's radical SZ which was developed in conjunction with coachbuilder Zagato and unveiled at the Geneva Salon in 1989.

Reprising a history of such co-operations between the two firms dating back to Zagato's body for the Alfa 6C 1500 of 1925, the project was based on a folio of initial sketches by Fiat stylist Robert Opron who came up with the idea of an aggressive-looking wedge-shaped, two-seater coupé based on the platform of Alfa Romeo's 75 saloon.

Opron's drawings were then fed into a computer, which tweaked the planes and angles in order to create the definitive body shape that was produced at the Zagato factory in Terrazzano di Rho, Lombardy.

The 'look' was very different from the Zagato-bodied cars of the 1950s and '60s, which were often instantly recognisable by their rounded, aerodynamic lines and were hand-crafted from aluminium. The SZ was shamelessly angular and featured panels made from lightweight, moulded plastic topped by an alloy roof.

To many, the car had a slightly home-made, kit-car appearance – but the shape was superbly aerodynamic and concealed a race/rally bred suspension set-up that endowed the SZ with tenacious roadholding and truly exceptional handling, helped by specially made Pirelli tyres and an almost absurdly low ride height (which could be increased hydraulically for tackling speed bumps and so on).

Under the bonnet, the car contained Alfa's rev-happy, 3-litre, quad camshaft V6 engine that drove the rear wheels through a five-speed, manual gearbox. Tuned to produce 210 horsepower, it offered sufficient grunt to propel the SZ to an exciting 152mph.

A genuine 'driver's car' that was quickly nicknamed 'Il Mostro' (the Monster), it featured six headlamps and an ostentatious rear wing that bisected a giant back window, while the interior offered a comprehensive, curved dashboard, leather-trimmed bucket seats and a surprisingly practical area for luggage.

Just 1,036 SZ's were made, all being left-hand-drive cars and all but one being finished in red with a grey roof and tan interior – the exception being the black car that was specially produced for Zagato boss Andrea Zagato.

Regular buyers who wanted more of a colour choice, however, were offered the options of red, yellow, black, silver or white when Alfa Romeo announced a convertible version of the car called the RZ – of which a mere 278 were ever built. Despite being outwardly similar, the RZ's bodywork comprised bespoke panels that were an entirely different shape to those used on its coupé stablemate.

Jaguar XJ220

Production dates: 1992 - 1994
Number built: 281
Designer: Jim Randall
Engine: 3.5 litre, V6
Fuel consumption: 18 mpg
Top speed: 152 mph

For a brief but glorious period before the arrival of the McLaren F1, Jaguar's remarkable XJ220 was the fastest production car in the world.

The brainchild of the marque's then director of engineering, Jim Randall, the XJ220 – named after its target top speed – began life as nothing more than a quarter-size cardboard model that Randall had created at home during the Christmas of 1987 and brought into work.

But rather than merely attracting the admiration of his colleagues (and Jaguar's bosses) the model served as a catalyst for a full-scale programme to create an operational concept car.

A team of volunteers agreed to help with the idea, which was developed with the assistance of the celebrated Jaguar tuner and racer Tom Walkinshaw who encouraged the use of the twin turbocharged, 3,500cc V6 engine that had already proved its worth in the XJR-10 and XJR-11 sports prototype competition cars – despite original thoughts of using a version of Jaguar's celebrated V12 unit mated to a four-wheel-drive system.

The original concept car (which did have a V12 engine) was completed at 3am on 18 October, 1988 and displayed at Birmingham's British International Motor Show just eight hours later – prompting a reaction from sufficient loyal and wealthy Jaguar fans to encourage the marque's management to consider putting the XJ220 into production.

A year later, the announcement was made that the car would, indeed, be built – and anyone interested should hand over a £50,000 deposit. The response was overwhelming, with many more times the number of people signing-up for the car than the quantity Jaguar had decided to build (220-350).

First deliveries were planned for 1992, by which time the V6 engine configuration with two-wheel-drive had been decided upon, reducing emissions, enabling a shorter wheelbase and saving production costs.

With a monocoque made from bonded aluminium topped with lightweight alloy bodywork, the XJ220 was one of the first road-going cars to feature a 'downforce' system to enhance its roadholding. It had the look of an extreme and futuristic endurance racer, but the interior was surprisingly luxurious with nicely trimmed leather bucket seats, electric windows, electrically heated door mirrors, air conditioning and green tinted glass.

The dashboard, meanwhile, curved behind the steering wheel and continued into the driver's door panel which accommodated an additional instrument pod containing four gauges, including a clock and a voltmeter.

In 1992, an early example of the car was taken to Italy's Nardi Ring where Jaguar's winner of the 1990 Le Mans 24 Hours, driver Martin Brundle, achieved a maximum speed of 217.1 mph. Despite requiring the removal of the catalytic converters and an adjustment to the standard rev limit setting, the speed was officially recognised as having been the fastest ever attained by a standard production car, leading the XJ220 to be featured in the *Guinness Book of World Records* from 1994 to 1999.

Despite the car's record breaking moment, however, the XJ220 was ultimately badly received. It attracted criticism for its size, lack of refinement, crude engine and poor visibility, with sales being further hampered by its arrival at the start of a recession. Although 350 cars had been planned, just 281 were built with a final selling price of around £150,000.

During the following decade, values plummeted by as much as two thirds with the XJ220 being sidelined by collectors in favour of cars such as the Ferrari F40 and McLaren F1. More recently, however, this oddity's place in modern automotive history has seen prices rise to over £300,000.

XJ220

JAGUAR
JAGUAR

Ferrari F512M

Production dates: 1994 - 1996
Number built: 501
Designer: Pininfarina
Engine: 4.9 litre flat 12
Fuel consumption: 18 mpg
Top speed: 195 mph

If you were a youth who loved cars during the 1980s, there's a good chance your bedroom wall would have been adorned with a poster of one of the era's most celebrated supercars – the Ferrari Testarossa. Wide, low and radically styled with its signature side strakes and single, high-level door mirror, it encapsulated a time when there was little shame attached to being outrageously flash.

Produced from 1984 until 1991, the Testarossa became something of a cult classic thanks, in part, to its appearance in the hit television series *Miami Vice* as the chosen wheels of actor Don Johnson's character Sonny Crockett.

Two Testarossas were delivered by the Italian marque as a result of Enzo Ferrari's alleged fury at seeing the first series in which Crockett drove a Corvette that had been mocked-up to look like a 1974 Ferrari Daytona Spider, attracting worldwide publicity for its a creator Tom McBurnie – whom the famously litigious Ferrari threatened to sue for fakery.

The two cars supplied for the show were originally black, but were soon repainted in dazzling white to make them more prominent in night scenes. One of them was put into storage in 1989 after the filming of the last episode, only to be re-commissioned in 2015 and later offered at auction with a mere 16,500 miles on the clock. It sold for a surprisingly modest $151,000.

The original Testarossa (meaning 'red head', for the colour of the flat-12 engine's cylinder heads) remained in production until 1991 when it was replaced by an improved version called the 512TR featuring a more powerful engine, smoother gearchange, repositioned drive train and mildly restyled bodywork.

The final, and best, iteration of the Testarossa, however, was the F512M, with the 'M' standing for Modificata. The engine was once more refined – notably with the use of a lighter crankshaft and titanium con rods to make it even more free-revving – while the most notable alteration to the bodywork involved the replacement of its predecessors' signature pop-up headlamps with fixed units.

With a mere 501 cars produced, the F512M was the rarest iteration of the Testarossa series, as well as being the fastest and the best handling. But, with a price tag of £130,000 it did not prove easy to sell and, within a decade, pre-owned examples with tiny mileages on the clock could be picked up for as little as £20,000.

As a result, one of the most radical, recognisable and usable Ferraris ever made looked set to become nothing more than a footnote in the marque's history.

In around 2010, however, collectors suddenly opened their eyes to the fact that these supercars with their flat 12 engines and 195mph top speeds, as well as Ferrari's celebrated 'gated' manual gearbox and those celebrated side strakes were absurdly undervalued and prices gradually began to climb. The result was that the auction markets suddenly became awash with F512Ms and their predecessors.

Prices initially soared to as much as £200,000 for the very finest examples – but they have since levelled to the point that a good one can now be had for less than half as much.

So, if you had the poster 30-odd years ago, maybe now is the time to buy the real thing?

F512M

Porsche 959

Production dates: 1987 - 1988 and 1992 - 1993
Number built: 300
Designer: Helmuth Bott
Engine: 2.85 litre, six cylinder
Fuel consumption: 18 mpg
Top speed: 197 mph

Like many of the world's most memorable supercars, the Porsche 959 was born with racing in mind. First mooted in 1981, it was originally intended to compete in the wild Group B rally class – meaning that at least 200 road-legal examples had to be built in order for the car to be homologated.

In the event, the 959 was never seriously campaigned as a rally car, instead becoming an experiment in technical innovation from which 300 lucky buyers would ultimately benefit.

The rarest and most sought after of all 959s were very much cars of the '90s, hence the model's appearance in this section of the book.

Often cited as the template on which virtually all supercars were based for years to come, the 959 used a 2.85 litre, six-cylinder engine which had already been developed and improved for use in various race classes.

It used a combination of water-cooled cylinder heads and air-cooled cylinder barrels and was fitted with a pair of sequential turbochargers to ensure a smooth flow of power rather than the famous 'all or nothing' delivery for which early Porsche Turbos had become infamous. The gearbox of the intended race car, meanwhile, combined five conventional forward gears with an additional 'off-road' gear to help on tricky terrain.

Indeed, one of the 959's many exceptional features was its ability to find traction in places where other cars would struggle – a result of Porsche's ingenious four-wheel-drive system, the Porsche-Steuer Kupplung or 'PSK' that electronically adjusted power distribution between the front and rear wheels according to the conditions.

Bodywork made from aluminium and Kevlar, a floor formed from fire-resistant Nomex and special hollow, magnesium alloy wheels with built-in tyre pressure sensors kept weight down to 1,450 kilos which, combined with the screaming engine's 444 horsepower, endowed the 959 with a top speed approaching 200 miles per hour – making it the fastest production car of its day.

The complexity of the design meant that the first cars were not delivered to customers until 1987, more than a year later than intended. But those who were patient enough to wait ended up with something of a bargain, since it is said that the £145,000 UK retail price of each 959 represented exactly half what it had cost to build.

Two versions were available: a more road-orientated model called 'Komfort' featuring leather upholstery, conventional seatbelts and luxuries such as a stereo system and air conditioning; and the racier (and rarer) 'Sport' that was supplied with a leather-wrapped roll cage, competition harnesses, cloth upholstery and an uprated suspension package. The stereo and air-con were deleted for the Sport, with the modifications trimming 100 kilos off the car's weight.

Between 1987 and 1988, just 292 959s were built, a mere 29 of which were 'Sport' versions. Only eight cars, all Komfort versions, were put together at the Stuttgart factory between 1992 and 1993 using left-over parts and were offered for sale only to Porsche's most favoured collectors at a price more akin to their build cost.

Now, more than 25 years later, they are worth at least £1.5 million apiece – and, like their late '80s forerunners, will still give virtually any present-day supercar a serious run for its money either on the track or on the road.

959 S

959 S
PORSCHE
959 S

PORSCHE

Lamborghini Diablo

Production dates: 1990 - 2000
Number built: 2,884
Designer: Marcello Gandini and Chrysler
Engine: 5.7 litre, 12 cylinder
Fuel consumption: 10 mpg
Top speed: Up to 202 mph

Having remained in production from 1974 to 1990 – during which time it had become steadily bigger, brasher, louder and more extreme – Lamborghini's celebrated Countach supercar had just about outstayed its welcome by the dawn of the new decade.

Its successor was the 'Diablo', another shamelessly aggressive, mid-engined road burner that was named after the Spanish world for 'devil' and proved to be the first Lamborghini capable of touching 200 mph, thanks to its aerodynamic shape and the fact that its V12, 5.7-litre powerplant churned out an enormous 485 horsepower without recourse to turbocharging.

Although distinctly Lamborghini in looks, its ultimate shape was not the sole work of the celebrated Marcello Gandini (who had previously created legendary Lambos such as the Miura, Countach and the Marzal concept car) but a joint effort between him and engineers at Chrysler, which had bought the 'raging bull' marque in 1987.

Gandini didn't approve of the finished article, although it continued the theme established with the Countach of having the driver and passenger mounted well forward towards the nose of the car to enable the engine and gearbox to be sited more or less in the middle of the chassis, thus providing optimum balance. A side effect of this arrangement was that driving the car felt somewhat akin to being in the cockpit of a fighter jet – an impression enhanced by the fact that the Diablo's high-mounted, slit-like rear window made it virtually impossible to see what was going on behind the car in an age long before reversing cameras became popular.

Going backwards slowly was, however, the exact opposite of what the Diablo was intended for. Its *raison d'etre* (as the Italians don't say) was all about going forwards quickly, something it was very good at.

To say this was a 'driver's car', however, would be an understatement. More accurately, it was a car for exceptionally stoic drivers who were prepared to put up with the weighty, non power-assisted steering, heavy clutch and brake pedals, booming exhaust note and the large amount of heat that poured off the engine and into the cabin whenever the Diablo was sitting in traffic.

The Diablo's specialist nature resulted in fewer than 3,000 cars being built during its 11-year production run, despite the fact that it was made available in several variations, such as the all-wheel-drive 'VT' version; the SE30 that celebrated Lamborghini's 30th anniversary by offering even more power and a stripped-down, race-inspired specification; and the limited edition, ultra-high performance SV (for Super Veloce).

The ultimate expression of the Diablo only came in 1999, however, after the firm had been taken over by Audi. Visually reworked by Luc Donckerwolke, it was made notably more civilised and less aggressive looking at the front, while the interior was made more comfortable for both driver and passenger.

The engine, meanwhile, was re-tuned to provide greater power with a more linear delivery – paving the way for the Diablo's replacement, the Murcielago, which was to take Lamborghini from being an ultra small volume maker of highly individual, difficult to drive, often temperamental cars that were loved and understood by the few to being a manufacturer of Teutonically engineered hypercars that were as easy to handle as a conventional saloon.

Some say that the essential Lamborghini character was lost along the way. But others appreciate the fact that having a raging bull on your bonnet no longer means you get out of the car feeling as though you've been wrestling with one...

Acknowledgements

Thanks are due to my friend, colleague and fellow old-car nut Robert Coucher for his eloquent foreword, and to the camera world's King of the Land Rover Nick Dimbleby and my Legendary Motorcycle Adventuring soul-mate Sam Pelly for their superb photographic contributions.

Most of all, however, thank you to my editor Andrew Whittaker and everyone at ACC Art Books for maintaining their endless patience and faith during the making of this tome which, due to my own lack of turbocharging, got off the line more in the style of the car on page 48 than the one on page 238...

Photo credits

P2-3 ©2017 Courtesy of RM Sotheby's; P4–5 Patrick Ernzen ©2015 Courtesy of RM Sotheby's; P6 Tom Wood ©2016 Courtesy of RM Sotheby's; P12-13 Khiem Pahm ©2011 Courtesy of RM Auctions; P15 Tom Wood ©2016 Courtesy of RM Sotheby's; P16-17 All: Darin Schnabel ©2015 Courtesy of RM Auctions; P19 Courtesy of RM Sotheby's; P20-21 All: Khiem Pahm ©2011 Courtesy of RM Auctions; P23 Courtesy of RM Sotheby's; P24-25 All: Josh Sweeney ©2016 Courtesy of RM Sotheby's; P27 Patrick Ernzen ©2015 Courtesy of RM Sotheby's; P28-29 Tim Scott ©2013 Courtesy of RM Sotheby's; P31 Courtesy of RM Sotheby's; P32-33 All: Courtesy of RM Sotheby's; P35 Darin Schnabel ©2017 Courtesy of RM Sotheby's; P36-37 Darin Schnabel ©2017 Courtesy of RM Sotheby's; P39 Courtesy of RM Sotheby's; P40-41 Courtesy of RM Sotheby's; P43 Gabor Mayer ©2017 Courtesy of RM Sotheby's; P44-45 All: Courtesy of RM Sotheby's; P46-47 Darin Schnabel ©2013 Courtesy of RM Auctions; P49 Courtesy of Bonhams; P50-51 All: Courtesy of Bonhams; P53 Patrick Ernzen ©2015 Courtesy of RM Sotheby's; P54-55 All: Patrick Ernzen ©2015 Courtesy of RM Sotheby's; P57 Nick Dimbleby; P58-59 All: Nick Dimbleby; P61 Tom Gidden ©2015 Courtesy of RM Auctions; P62-63 All: Tom Gidden ©2015 Courtesy of RM Auctions; P65 Courtesy of Bonhams; P66-67 All: Courtesy of Bonhams; P69 Peter Singhof ©2018 Courtesy of RM Sotheby's; P70-71 Peter Singhof ©2018 Courtesy of RM Sotheby's; P72-73 All: Peter Singhof ©2018 Courtesy of RM Sotheby's; P75 Robin Adams ©2014 Courtesy of RM Auctions; P76-77 All: Robin Adams ©2014 Courtesy of RM Auctions; P78-79 Robin Adams ©2014 Courtesy of RM Auctions; P81 Patrick Ernzen ©2012 Courtesy of RM Auctions; P82-83 All: ©2018 Courtesy of RM Auctions; P84-85 Tim Scott/Fluid Images ©2010 Courtesy of RM Auctions; P87 Patrick Ernzen ©2015 Courtesy of RM Sothebys; P88-89 Left: Ryan Merrill ©2017 Courtesy of RM Sotheby's, Top Right: Patrick Ernzen ©2015 Courtesy of RM Sotheby's, Bottom Right: Patrick Ernzen ©2015 Courtesy of RM Sotheby's; P90-91 Patrick Ernzen ©2015 Courtesy of RM Sotheby's; P93 Courtesy RM Sotheby's; P94-95 All: Martyn Goddard; P97 Tim Scott ©2015 Courtesy of RM Sotheby's; P98-99 Tim Scott ©2015 Courtesy of RM Sotheby's; P100-101 All: Tim Scott ©2015 Courtesy of RM Sotheby's; P103 Courtesy of Bonhams; P104-105 All: Courtesy of Bonhams; P107 Darin Schnabel ©2013 Courtesy of RM Auctions; P108 Darin Schnabel ©2013 Courtesy of RM Auctions; P109 All: Courtesy of RM Auctions; P110-111 Brandon Sullivan ©2018 Courtesy of RM Auctions; P113 Courtesy of RM Sotheby's; P114-115 All: Courtesy of RM Sotheby's; P117 David Bush ©2016 Courtesy of RM Sotheby's; P118-119 David Bush ©2016 Courtesy of RM Sotheby's; P121 Courtesy of Bonhams; P122-123 All: Courtesy of Bonhams; P124-125 DS Automobiles; P126-127 Darin Schnabel ©2014 Courtesy of RM Auctions; P129 Darin Schnabel ©2010 Courtesy of RM Auctions; P130-131 All: Courtesy of RM Sotheby's; P133 Courtesy RM Sotheby's; P134-135 All: Corey Silvia ©2015 Courtesy of RM Sotheby's; P137 Photographer: Harvey Smith, Courtesy of RM Sotheby's; P138-139 All: Photographer: Harvey Smith, Courtesy of RM Sotheby's; P140-141 Darin Schnabel ©2014 Courtesy of RM Auctions; P143 Patrick Ernzen ©2016 Courtesy of RM Sotheby's; P144-145 Patrick Ernzen ©2016 Courtesy of RM Sotheby's; P146-147 All: ©2017 Courtesy of RM Sotheby's; P149 Erik Fuller ©2018 Courtesy of RM Sotheby's; P150-151 All: Erik Fuller ©2018 Courtesy of RM Sotheby's; P153 Courtesy of Bonhams; P154-155 Courtesy of Bonhams; P157 ©TedisGraphic | Theodore W. Pieper Courtesy of RM Sotheby's; P158-159 All: ©TedisGraphic | Theodore W. Pieper Courtesy of RM Sotheby's; P160-161 Darin Schnabel ©2013 Courtesy of RM Auctions; P163 Darin Schnabel © 2010 Courtesy RM Sotheby's; P164-165 shooterz.biz ©2010 Courtesy of RM Auctions; P166-167 Patrick Ernzen ©2015 Courtesy of RM Sotheby's; P169 Jack Passey ©2017 Courtesy of RM Sotheby's; P170-171 All: Jack Passey ©2017 Courtesy of RM Sotheby's; P172-173 Jack Passey ©2017 Courtesy of RM Sotheby's; P175 David Bush ©2017 Courtesy of RM Sotheby's; P176-177 David Bush ©2017 Courtesy of RM Sotheby's; P178-179 All: David Bush ©2017 Courtesy of RM Sotheby's; P181 Courtesy of RM Sotheby's; P182-183 Remi Dargegan ©2018 Courtesy of RM Sotheby's; P185 Courtesy of RM Sotheby's; P186-187 Courtesy of RM Sotheby's; P188-189 Sam Pelly; P191 Gabor Mayer Courtesy of RM Sotheby's; P192-193 Courtesy of RM Sotheby's; P195 Patrick Ernzen ©2015 Courtesy of RM Sotheby's; P196-197 Patrick Ernzen © Courtesy of RM Sotheby's; P199 Tom Wood ©2015 Courtesy of RM Auctions; P200-201 All: Cymon Taylor ©2016 Courtesy of RM Sotheby's; P203 Darlin Schnabel ©2016 Courtesy of RM Sotheby's; P204-205 Darlin Schnabel ©2016 Courtesy of RM Sotheby's; P206-207 All: Darlin Schnabel ©2016 Courtesy of RM Sotheby's; P208-209 Darin Schnabel ©2016 Courtesy of RM Sotheby's; P211 Teddy Pieper ©2014 Courtesy of RM Auctions; P212-213 All: Teddy Pieper ©2014 Courtesy of RM Auctions; P215 Courtesy of RM Sotheby's; P216-217 Courtesy of RM Sotheby's; P219 Patrick Ernzen ©2015 Courtesy of RM Sotheby's; P220-221 Patrick Ernzen ©2015 Courtesy of RM Sotheby's; P222-223 Courtesy of RM Sotheby's; P225 Tom Wood ©2016 Courtesy of RM Sotheby's; P226-227 All: Tom Wood ©2016 Courtesy of RM Sotheby's; P229 Tim Scott ©2016 Courtesy of RM Sotheby's; P230-231 All: Tim Scott ©2016 Courtesy of RM Sotheby's; P232-233 Erik Fuller ©2015 Auctions America; P235 Darin Schnabel ©2016 Courtesy of RM Sotheby's; P236-237 All: Darin Schnabel ©2016 Courtesy of RM Sotheby's; P239 Erik Fuller ©2016 Courtesy of RM Sotheby's; P240-241 All: Erik Fuller ©2016 Courtesy of RM Sotheby's; P243 Manchester Capri Club; P244-245 Manchester Capri Club; P246-247 Phil Talbot / Alamy Stock Photo; P248-249 Courtesy of RM Sotheby's; P251 Courtesy of RM Sotheby's; P252-253 All: Patrick Ernzen ©2015 Courtesy of RM Sotheby's; P255 Courtesy of Honda; P256-257 Courtesy of Honda; P259 Courtesy of Bonhams; P260-261 All: Courtesy of Bonhams; P263 Cymon Taylor 2015 © RM Sotheby's; P264-265 Cymon Taylor 2015 © RM Sotheby's; P267 Darin Schnabel ©2016 Courtesy of RM Sotheby's; P268-269 All: Darin Schnabel ©2016 Courtesy of RM Sotheby's; P270-271 Patrick Ernzen ©2015 Courtesy of RM Sotheby's; P273 Cymon Taylor ©2018 Courtesy of RM Sotheby's; P274-277 All: Jeremy Cliff ©2015 Courtesy of RM Sotheby's; P279 Remi Dargegen ©2016 Courtesy of RM Sotheby's; P280-281 All: Remi Dargegen ©2016 Courtesy of RM Sotheby's; P283 Erik Fuller ©2018 Courtesy of RM Sotheby's; P284-285 All: Erik Fuller ©2018 Courtesy of RM Sotheby's

Cover Illustration: The Mercedes-Benz 190SL might not be universally loved, but its stylish roadster body – based on the faster, more glamorous 300SL – epitomises the free thinking that inspired automotive designers of the 1950s and 60s to create some of the most interesting, exciting and innovative cars the world has ever seen. This book aims to bring together a non-definitive selection of such designs from that golden era and the few decades before and after it that succeeded in combining innovation with aesthetic appeal in such a way that they truly deserve to be called 'classics'.

ISBN 978-1-85149-916-8

First published by ACC Art Books in 2018
Reprinted 2020, 2022, 2023, 2025

A CIP catalogue record for this book is available from the British Library

EU GPSR Authorised Representative:
Easy Access System Europe Oü, 16879218
Address: Mustamäetee 50, 10621 Tallinn, Estonia
Email: gpsr@easproject.com Tel: +358 40 5003575

Printed in China by C&C Offset Printing Co. Ltd
for ACC Art Books Ltd, Woodbridge, Suffolk, UK

www.accartbooks.com